TEALING

THE

GATEWAY TO A

CW00456098

By

Sandra J Burke DPA, MCIM, MIPD

Published by Tealing Community Council – Contact: editor@tealingvillage.org

www.tealingvillage.org

First published June 2000 © Tealing Community Council and the contributors.
Design and Production by AM Graphics, Glenrothes
Printed in Scotland

1

PREFACE

In the year of the millennium, the people of Tealing wanted to celebrate their heritage, record the past and share their pride in the area with others. And so, the idea for this book and the permanent photographic exhibition in Tealing Hall, was born. The response has been amazing. Folk, who have lived here past and present, have searched their lofts and cub by-holes for old press cuttings, photographs and other memorabilia. Local community groups have rallied around. The guides have acted as roving reporters, interviewing their elders and unearthing their fondest memories. The children of Tealing Primary School have produced work for the book and the exhibition. Many of their parents, teachers, the minister, the local policeman and other villagers, have all helped.

Special thanks go to the members of the Tealing Millennium Celebration Planning Group, all of whom have given freely of their time over a long period. They are Sandra Burke (Chairperson), Janet Stewart (Secretary), Moira Paton (Treasurer), Bessie Coventry, Agnes Ramsay, Margaret Thomson, Margaret Mitchell, Ruby Burke, Graeme and Jackie Reoch, Lynn Hally and Charles Wilson. For their practical help with the book and the exhibition, appreciation is also extended to the Reverend Sydney Graham, Head Teacher Miss Linda Hendry, Bishop E Luscombe, William and Jessie Wilkie, Eva Scott, Jessie Mudie, Charles and Margaret Young, Graham and May Thomson, Chris Allan, Kay Dennis, Andy Thomson, Mrs Eisler and Miss E Bowie.

The following organisations have also assisted; Tealing Community Council; Tealing Primary School, Tealing Hall Committee, Angus Council Archive Unit and other departments, Dundee City Council Archive Unit and Local Studies Library, Tealing WRI, Tealing Women's Guild, the Margaret Napier School of Dancing, Tealing Wednesday Club, Tealing Guides, Tealing Primary School PTA, Tealing School Board, Auchterhouse/Murroes/Tealing Parish Church and Maxwelltown Dog Training Club.

A special mention must go to Eva Scott for researching and collating the memories of so many local residents, many of whom are acknowledged in later chapters. Such was the tremendous response that it has not been possible to use all of the material in this book, but every statement will be catalogued, and preserved for the future, in a village archive. We are indebted to everyone who responded.

This is a community project, started off by Tealing Community Council, but completed with the help of many others. In the course of preparing the and exhibition, our community spirit has been re-energised. If we can sustain that energy, it will have been even more worthwhile than expected.

All of the information contained in this book has been received and used in good faith and has been researched, as far as possible, to ensure accuracy. The views expressed are not necessarily those of the publishers.

INTRODUCTION

Every week, tens of thousands of people travel through Tealing. Few of them realise it, for most of them are in vehicles driving on the mighty A 90, the main arterial route north from Perth to Aberdeen. Tealing sits astride the dual carriageway just a few miles north of the city of Dundee. It is the first Angus settlement encountered on the A90 travelling north, often called "The Gateway to Angus".

But it is so much more than a gateway. Tealing is a vibrant rural community with a rich and colourful past. From the early Pictish settlement, to its important place in Scotland's religious history, through to the role of the aerodrome during the second world war, Tealing has much to tell that is of interest to a wider audience.

For generations, Tealing has attracted visitors and ramblers from Dundee, Angus and beyond. They are attracted to the outstanding landscape and rolling countryside at the foot of the Sidlaws in the shadow of Craigowl. Some of them come to see the old church, the Dovecot and the Earthhouse. Many cycle, run or walk in the area for recreation or are on their way to "picnic in the Sidlaws" -an age-old pastime for Dundonians. But few of them really know the place. If Angus is Scotland's best kept secret, Tealing may well be the best kept secret in Angus. The five hundred or so people who live in Tealing know all about its attractions. Day in and day out they enjoy the peace and quiet of rural living found in this lovely part of Scotland.

This book begins to tell the story of Tealing. It is not exhaustive and it is as detailed as we can hope to be within the time and resources available. We hope that it will hold something of interest for everyone -for residents, for visitors and for the just plain curious!

CONTENTS

DID You KNOW?

As a taster of what is to follow, here are some interesting wee snippets that you might not have known about Tealing.

One of the earliest known pieces of old Scots inscription existing anywhere in Scotland, dated 1380, is preserved within Tealing Church.

Alexander Maxwell of Tealing was charged with reset and helping a thief in 1553. This was bad enough, but he was the local magistrate at the time!

Patrick Scrymsoure of Tealing married into the Coutts banking family (bankers to the current royal family) in 1761.

The Maxwelltown area of Dundee was named after the Tealing Maxwells who once owned the upper part of the Hilltown. About 1780, David Maxwell arranged that local streets should be named after members of his family. This accounts for Ann, Eliza, George, Alexander, Elizabeth and William Street.

Sir Stewart Duke-Elder, born in Tealing in 1898, operated on the Prime Minister Ramsay McDonald in 1932 and was appointed surgeon oculist to King Edward VIII, King George VI and Queen Elizabeth 11.

David Goodfellow, of the Goodfellow & Steven bakery family, farmed Balnuith in Tealing from 1929 until 1944.

The Russian Foreign Minister, Molotov, landed at Tealing Airfield in 1942 on his way to a meeting with Winston Churchill to sign the Anglo-Russian Treaty.

Tealing farmers provided large quantities of peas for Smedleys from 1947 until 1972.

The actor A Mungall, of Z Cars and Dr Who fame, was flagged down on the main road by the Tealing Bobby, David Oram, in the 1960's and told to "follow that motor bike!" The motor bike had been stolen and they got their man.

The author, Rosamunde Pilcher is married to Graham Pilcher, great grandson of jute baron William who was the uncle of the late Edmund C Cox who once owned Tealing House.

McIntosh Patrick painted" The Road to Tealing" in the late eighties, as a gift for a friend who lives locally.

CHAPTER 1
TEALING "COUNTRY OF BROOKS OR WATERS"
EARLY HISTORY; THE FIRST 1000 YEARS

The stunning backdrop of the Sidlaw hills was shaped 375 million years ago. Carved by glaciers as the ice retreated through glacial meltwater erosion, several smaller channels were scored on the hills. In the flatlands below, the largely populated of Tealing sit at 350 feet above sea level, reaching 1492 feet at the summit of Craigowl.

The area of Angus that we know of as Tealing today is bounded by Inverarity and Glamis to the north, the Murroes to the east, Auchterhouse to the west and Strathmartine and Dundee to the south and covers an area of approximately 15 square miles. It is a fertile place where several small streams, the largest of which is the Fithie, provide natural drainage and moisture for the crops.

Tealing Earth-House.

It is hard to say when people first started living in the Tealing area. We know that there were settlers on the banks of the Tay as long ago as 4000 BC in the Neolithic age, but their lives were hard and, as mere survival presented a problem, they left very few relics. In Angus, there is also some evidence of Neolithic and early Bronze Age burials.

Tealing has several ancient relics. J Romilly Allen, FSA Scotland, described Tealing in his paper "Notice of Prehistoric Remains near Tealing in Forfarshire" dated 16 February 1881, as a district "very rich" in prehistoric remains. These include the cup-marked boulder in Tealing Wood, the cup-marked stone at Cross House, Balkemback and the "circle of stones" or "supposed Druidical temple" at Balkemback Wood. Romilly Allen stated that these cup-marked stones were similar to those found on Ilkley Moor in Yorkshire. They are thought to date to the Bronze Age circa 1800 BC and, since they also exist in Sweden, are thought to be evidence of ornamentation of rocks by migrating Nordic peoples. However, others have attributed them to religious practices or even to crude representations of planetary movement.

The earliest evidence of settlement in Tealing is the earth-house or souterrain in the field at Tealing Home farm. It is one of the largest of such structures, found in the north of

Scotland and also known as Eirde houses, Picts' houses or Weems. The Tealing earthhouse probably dates to 100 or 200 AD. Not long before that, Scotland had started to come out of the Iron Age, with the rest of Europe, between 27 BC and AD 68, when the Romans brought literacy and a radical new way of life to Britain. When uncovered in

1871, Tealing earth-house contained a range of artefacts on the floor of the structure, including pottery, bronze rings, several saddle querns (used for grinding grain) and a few fragments of Roman pottery and glass.

Historic Scotland maintains Tealing soutterain and advises that it would have been used for the storage of grains and other foodstuffs. Its size is such that it may have served several local farming communities or have been used to store grain destined for the Roman Army. The settlers most probably lived alongside the earth-house in a timber thatched building above ground. So, if we accept that the earth-house was the first evidence of group settlement in the area, Tealing is almost two thousand years old.

What was going on in Tealing over the next few hundred years is a bit of a mystery. We know that Tealing is within the area that was ruled by the Picts, the group of tribal peoples known to be living north of the Forth, and throughout what is now the north of Scotland, from circa 100AD to the mid -ninth century. The people who lived alongside Tealing earth-house and elsewhere in this area at that time were almost certainly Picts. If our earth-house, as suspected by Historic Scotland, provided grain for the Roman Army, how can this be? For we know that the Picts were fiercely hostile to the Romans. Did the Romans commandeer Tealing earth-house? We will never know.

As depicted at the excellent Pictavia Visitor Centre in Brechin, the mysterious Picts were farmers, craftspeople, hunters and warriors who were largely converted to Christianity between the fifth and seventh centuries. They developed a superb and highly original art that chiefly survives in the form of sculptured stones, many of which can still be seen in and around Angus. One such stone remains at Balluderon, also known as St Martin's Stone. Although it is broken and only the four-foot high lower section survives, it depicts a relief carved horseman and is considered unusual because it is decorated on one face only. St Martin's Stone is also, reputedly, one of the stones that relates the famous legend of the Nine Maidens.

St. Martin's Stone, Balluderon.
Courtesy of Alistair D. Carty.

The Romans arrived in Britain in 55BC, conquered Britannia from 43AD and in 84AD Julius Agricola won a victory in the Pictish heartland over the" Caledonians", killing

7

10,000 men. The Roman victory was not repeated. They were unable to hold positions so far north and eventually retreated to build Hadrian's Wall and Antonines Wall, to hold the marauding northerners back. Pictland was then relatively "free" within Roman Britannia for many years, although periodic raids by the Picts and the Scots of Ireland continued to harry the Romans who called them "barbarians who were creating havoc". In 368, the Pict, Scot and Saxon tribes attacked the Romans in London, plundering their treasures. By 410 the Romans had left Britain for good.

The Pictish kings continued to reign in this part of Scotland. On 20 May 685, not far from here on the plains of Dunnichen in Angus, Bridei, King of the Picts faced the "invincible" Anglo-Saxon force that had occupied Southern Pictland for the previous 30 years. The Picts won that day and massacred the entire English Anglo-Saxon host, including their king. It is said, that had Bridei lost that great battle, the Scotland of today would not exist and all of Britain might have become English. When Bridei's grandson, King Brude, died in 706 King Nechtan succeeded him. This brings us back to the Tealing connection.

In 710 AD, Nechtan sent a messenger to Ceolfrid, Abbot of the Monastery at Jarrow, seeking information regarding the timing of Easter and asking that architects be sent to him to build "a church in the Roman manner". Ceolfrid was delighted that Nechtan was willing to embrace the Roman Church in favour of the Celtic Church and he despatched the papal missionary, St Boniface, to Angus. St Boniface established churches at Felin (Tealing), Invergowrie and Restenneth. The church in Tealing was dedicated to St Peter. We don't know exactly where in Tealing this first church stood. Epitaph historian Mr A Jervise, writing in 1879, thought it had been located on a rising just yards north of Tealing House. However, in 1880, historian Alex J Warden said that this was a mistake. There had been a chapel on that spot north of Tealing House, but the remains of it had long since been removed. Warden thought that the site of the ancient church had most probably been on the site of the present church, but he could not be sure.

The Picts continued to rule in Angus and the north of Scotland, through the invasion of the Vikings in 794, and until around 843, when Kenneth MacAlpin united the Picts and the Scots as one nation under his rule. This was the first step in creating a united Scotland, a process not completed until at least 1034 and perhaps much later. The next mention of Tealing in the annals of history is between 1159 and 1163 when Restenneth Priory (by Forfar) was made a cell of the Abbey of Jedburgh. By Charter, King Malcolm IV, commonly called "Malcolm the Maiden", granted the priory, amongst others, the churches of Crachnatharact, Pethefrin, Teleth (Tealing), Duninath, Dyserth and Egglespether. Then, in 1174, Hugh Giffard of Tealing was recorded as one of the hostages for the release of King William (the Lion) of Scotland. King William had been captured by King Henry 11of England and sent to prison in a castle at Falaise in Normandy. In return for his freedom,

Henry 11 extracted an oath of allegiance from William that Henry was his feudal superior. It was known as the Treaty of Falaise and it was a humiliation for Scotland that lasted for 15 years until William renegotiated the return of his powers and lands from Henry's successor, Richard the Lionheart. It may have been for this service to King William that Hugh Giffard was bestowed the grant of Tealing in the late 12th century.

The name Tealing comes from the Gaelic, meaning "country of streams and waters" The exact date that Tealing became the accepted name for the area is unclear, for the history books show that several different versions were used through the ages -Felin, Tellein, Thelin, Tellone, Teleth, Telen and Telyn are all mentioned. By the 17th century, the use of "Tealing" appears to have been well established ..

CHAPTER 2 THE CHURCH

To a large extent, the church has defined Tealing's place in history. Most of the villages of Angus started off as parishes within or encompassing the large private estates. And, since it was the Kirk, the Estates and the old School Board that kept the best records, what we know of distant times is a story that weaves its way back and fore between each of them. Almost every step of the way, at least until recent times, the Church has been pivotal in the development of Tealing.

EARLY HISTORY

As mentioned in the opening chapter, our first and ancient church was built around 710AD by St Boniface, the papal missionary who, over his lifetime, founded around 150 churches in the north of Scotland. The first three were at Invergowrie, Tealing and Restenneth. Various scholars and historians have pondered where the original church was built. Most of them think it likely that it was on the current site, so there may well have been several churches there before the present church built around 1808. The foundations are most likely ancient and there are certainly relics within the church that pre-date the building of the church by several hundred years. We know that these must have come from the previous church (or churches) and we can imagine the builders carefully salvaging and preserving these elements for re-use. The gravestones in the churchyard that are still legible date as far back as the 16th century and we have records of the parish Ministers from 1561.

The timeline at the back of this book sets out the significant dates in Tealing's history and lists, where known, the names of the Ministers appointed over the years. Beyond that, this chapter elaborates on the most significant elements of our church history. We begin in 1199. Not long after that, ancient records show that the Priory of St Andrews is to hold the land of Pitpointie, which had also been gifted to it by Hugh Giffard of Tealing, as long as it holds the Church of Tealing. The Priest's Croft may have been what is now the farm of Prieston, about one mile north-west of the church. The last-mentioned deed contains a provision that William, the son of Hugh Giffard, shall pay three merks yearly for his father's kitchen, and shall clothe his father till he assumes the habit of a cannon. He was also bound to pay for his father's four servants. After these gifts had been made, but prior to 1275, the Church of Telyn was disjoined from the diocese of St Andrews and annexed to the diocese of Dunkeld, and ever afterwards it belonged to that diocese. In Roman Catholic, and ever afterwards in Episcopal times, the parson of Tealing held the office of Archdeacon of Dunkeld Cathedral.

RARE INSCRIPTIONS

Two ancient inscriptions, still contained within Tealing Church confirm this. Firstly +HEYR lyis Ingram of maystr in arit ercdene of made in his xxxii yhere prayis for hym yat hafand lx blank space) yherys of elyd in the yher of cryst Mrcccilxxx (a blank It would seem that this slab was inscribed during his lifetime and that spaces were left for the year of his death. It is one of the oldest existing inscriptions in Scotland, and is remarkable for being in the vernacular of the country. Writing in 1880, Alex Warden, author of Angus or Forfarshire, The Lands and the People, said, "no other inscription of the same kind is known to exist in the kingdom". The inscription shows that Ingram, born in 1320, was made "ercdene"in 1352. There may have been some relationship between him and a contemporary priest, Robert De Kethenis, who was recommended in 1345 by mandate from Pope Clement IV to the Abbots of Arbroath and Cupar. The family de Kethenis were early settled in Kettins and it is probable that Ingram and Robert may both have been descendants of that old family, whose lands appear to have been given off to the Ogilvys about the time when these two churchmen were born.

The second inscription is on the tombstone of Archdeacon John Ramsay who died on 10 May 1618. John Ramsay was born in 1569 and was educated at the University of St Andrews where he obtained an MA in 1587. He became Minister at Tealing in 1590 and described the parish as "has much pepull and requiring an able person to travel in the function of this

Tombstone of Archdeacon John Ramsay.
Courtesy of D. C. Thomson & Co. Ltd.

ministrie". His tombstone is large and magnificent, depicting him as a bearded ecclesiastic (half-life size) reading at a desk or lectern. In one corner is a shield with the Ramsay arms and surmounted with the legend, "VIVIT POST FYNE RA and in the corner opposite are the words 10 DIE MAIl 1618 AE 49"In an article for the Evening in March 1984, The Rev Bob Johnstone said "it is in excellent condition showing the Archdeacon in full clerical dress. There's nothing like it in Scotland, it is a real find." In 1880, it was also noted that there was a tombstone on the floor of the church with a Latin that translates "erected to the memory of Mr Ramsay, Archdeacon of Doctor of Divinity, for 35 years a most watchful pastor of this Church, by his sorrowing widow, Elizabeth Kinloch".

THE REVEREND JOHN GLAS AND THE "GLASSITES"

Without doubt, Tealing's most famous Minister was the Reverend John Glas. He was born in Fife in 1695 and came from a family of Ministers. He studied at the universities of St Andrews and Edinburgh and in 1719, shortly after he was first licensed to preach, he became Minister at Tealing. In 1721 he married Catherine Black, daughter of the Rev John Black of Perth.

Soon after his ordination he began to vent opinions, then strange in Scotland, regarding the National Covenants, the relationship between the Church and the State and the right of the latter to interfere in matters of religion. His views brought him into direct conflict with the Church Courts and caused a schism that reverberated throughout Scotland. On 13 July 1725, he formed a society of 74 persons to exercise discipline and hold monthly celebration of Communion in his preferred manner. Since such heresies could not be connived at, he was brought to the bar of his Presbytery in 1727 to explain himself. He made an honest and explicit statement of his views and denied the divine authority of the Presbyterian form of Church government. His Presbytery suspended him in April 1728 and after long process, his views led first to his suspension by Synod, and ultimately in March 1730, to deposition by the Commission of the General Assembly.

In the same year, he set up an independent congregation in Dundee, supported by families from Tealing including Baxter, the jute manufacturer. He gave his name to his followers, who became known as "the Glassites". In 1733 he went to Perth, where he opened a church in the face of much opposition. He was joined there by a young man Robert Sandeman, who became his son-in-law, and from whom the sect is better known in England and America as the "Sandemanians". John Glas then ministered in Edinburgh, finally returning to Dundee.

During his lifetime the demise of his son Captain George Glas and his family devastated him. Captain Glas, born in 1725, made several voyages to the West Coast of Africa and the Canary Islands. In 1765, aged 40, he was "thrust through the body from behind" by mutineers on board their ship heading back to London. His wife and daughter begged for mercy, but they were thrown overboard and drowned. A chronicler later described it thus "the death of his son, daughter and granddaughter was the most remarkable trial whichever befel Mr Glas".

The Rev, James Glas died on 2 Nov 1773 in Dundee, aged 78. He had survived his wife and all of their fifteen children. Mr and Mrs Glas were interred in the same grave in the Howff, Dundee, and nine of their children lie beside their parents.

That a small village like Tealing was connected with such a remarkable series of events is surprising enough, but one other of our Ministers was also an apostatising clergyman. The reverend Walter Tait was Minister of Tealing Parish Church from 1797 to 1813, when he transferred to Trinity College, Edinburgh. He was afterwards charged with heresy and, being convicted, was deposed by the General Assembly. He founded a sect that became known as the Catholic Apostolic Church. An observer later wrote "these cases showed strong dissenting, schismatic proclivities in a small and rather sequestered parish, where they would not very readily have been expected; but the unity of the parish did not suffer any very serious or permanent damage from them".

THE STATISTICAL ACCOUNTS

Parish Ministers were also the writers of the records of Tealing Parish for input to the. Statistical Accounts of Scotland -in 1790 (Rev. John Gellatly), 1836 (Rev. David B Mellis) and 1968 (Rev. James Kidd). The Statistical Accounts were the idea of Sir John Sinclair, who, between 1791 and 1798, arranged for the publication of an account of every parish in Scotland to be drawn up by its Minister. He was also a Member of Parliament and he described the initiative as "an enquiry into the state of the country for the purpose of ascertaining the quantum of happiness enjoyed by its inhabitants and the means of future improvement". These" snapshots" of parish life have provided many historians, economists and sociologists with useful information.

Writing about the church in 1790, the Rev John Gellatly said "the church is of very ancient foundation. A few fragments of carved stones seem to indicate that the original church was an elegant gothic structure, but the present fabric, however, bears no mark of antiquity and is but indifferent both to style and condition. The stipend is about 2000 merks Scots, exclusive of the manse and garden; as to the glebe, it would be, as it generally is in the country, rather a disadvantage, if the incumbent had not been so lucky as to get a small farm. The Crown is patron. The average number of scholars at the parochial school is only about 30, owing to the badness of the roads here in the winter season, and the nearness of the skirts of the parish to the schools of the parishes around. At present there is not one beggar".

In September 1836, Rev. David B Mellis, wrote of Tealing's ecclesiastical state" the parish church and the manse are nearly in the centre of the parish, and whether distance or population be considered, a more eligible situation for them could not have been chosen. The church was built about the year 1806 and contains sittings for 700 individuals. The manse was built around 1803 and has undergone such alterations, and received such repairs, as make it very comfortable. The extent of the glebe is five

and its annual value may be estimated at L14. As to the stipend, it is 10 chalders, and L30. There is not any place for public worship in the parish except the Established Church, and all the inhabitants of the parish, with the exception of four or five individuals, adhere to the establishment. The average number of communicants is about 450. The average amount of church collections yearly is about L50".

Regarding the poor, he continued "the average number of persons receiving parochial aid is 10 (out of a population of 766) and the average sum allotted to each per month is 5 or 6 shillings; but, besides those persons who receive statedly parochial aid, there are some to whom money, according to their circumstances is occasionally given; and a considerable sum is annually expended on fuel and clothing."

THE FREE CHURCH AND THE DISRUPTION

In 1843, there was a third breakaway from the Established Church in Scotland. This was the "Disruption" associated with Thomas Chalmers and led to the formation of the Free Church. Over 400 ministers resigned from the Church of Scotland. The Minister of the Parish, David Barclay Mellis, and almost the entire congregation, "came out" in 1843. A church was erected forthwith, up the Huntingfaulds Road, and the manse soon afterwards. (The manse still stands and is now privately owned, the church ruins are in the garden). The Free Church also provided schools for their children. The County Register of Free Church Clergy and Teachers in 1845 shows that the teacher in Tealing was a Mr William Rattray.

William Elder became Minister of Tealing Parish Church in 1843 and although he "subscribed the Solemn Engagement and both series of Resolutions of Convocation" he did not join the Free Church. He took up the charge at Tealing on 28 September 1843, with a much-reduced congregation, where he remained until he died in August 1890. When David Mellis died in 1861, he was succeeded at Tealing Free Church by Duncan Turner, who ministered there until 1883, when the Rev, Neil S Elder took over. So, there was a time, between 1883 and 1889, when the Ministers of both Tealing Churches were known as "the Rev. Elder" - very confusing!

The History of the Free Church Congregations states that "the church suffered through the extinction of handloom weaving and the absorption of crofts in larger farms". Then, in 1900, the Free Church united with the United Presbyterian Church to become the United Free Church. In 1929, the United Free Church united with the Established Church (the Church of Scotland) and Tealing returned to having one church, Tealing Parish Church. The Rev. James Alexander Sutherland Wilson took over the reins at Tealing on 15 June 1929, the 86 year separation of the congregations over. The United Free Church, manse and outbuildings were sold for £845, 9 shillings and the proceeds were invested for the Fabric Fund.

Two LUSTY ANGELS

Writing in 1880, Alex Warden in "Angus In Parishes -Tealing" said "in the front wall of the church there is an old sculptured stone, upon which is portrayed a sea serpent. The mason who built the stone into the wall had not been acquainted with sea serpents, as it is placed upside down. On the back wall there are two lusty angels, but this is not a very old stone, and the sculptor not an artist of merit. High up on the west gable there is an elaborately sculptured stone with several figures upon it. They appear to be administering rites in connection with some Episcopal service. It is beautiful executed".

THE 20TH CENTURY

In 1889 Samuel Macaulay became Minister of Tealing Parish Church, where he remained until he died in 1925. Rev. Macaulay was very active in the Parish and his name shows up regularly in the School Board Minutes. He is also mentioned in the 1909 poem "The Tealing Bazaar" by H Lamont "Mrs Martin and spouse and parson Macaulay, a' footed it oot o'er the floor gay and brawly".

In 1921, he presided over the much more serious affair of the Dedication of the War Memorial. The Dundee Advertiser on 29 August 1921 reported "from every part of the parish of Tealing came little parties on Saturday afternoon to be present at the unveiling of their war memorial. It was an afternoon of intermittent sun and shadow, and the scene presented there in the kindly shelter of purple-crowned Craigowl, though simple, was none the less deeply impressive. The school children formed a choir round the base of the monument and their sweet young voices rose on the perfumed air with those of their elders in harmonious psalms of thanksgiving for the sacred memories of those who had fallen. Rev Macaulay, in an eloquent address, said that, in reply to the frequent inquiry why such a quiet rural parish required a war memorial, he desired to say that the war had sent it's call into every hamlet and village in the land, and that in proportion to their numbers, the small parishes had contributed as liberally of their manhood and womanhood as the larger ones, and had suffered as great and sore losses. The clear notes of the Last Post were blown by Bugler Robert Smith of the Black Watch".

NUMBERS DECLINE

On 1st December 1963, Tealing Parish Church was linked with Murroes under the ministry of the Rev. James Kidd. Rev Kidd had transferred to Tealing just over a year earlier, in April 1962. In the 1967 Statistical Account he wrote" church-going has declined for several reasons, though nominal membership stands at 360, public worship is usually attended by 50-60, and about 240 attend Holy Communion. The centre of population has moved from the Kirkton and workers have more free time, whereas, in the past, Sunday was the only day when friends could meet at church".

On 14 December 1982, the congregations of Murroes and Tealing held a service of union in Tealing Church. The united congregations were to be known as Murroes and Tealing and would, thereafter, worship in Murroes Church. The Manse was to remain in Tealing, where it still is today, and Rev. Kidd would be the Minister of the united charge until a new minister was inducted and he could retire. At this time some of the Tealing members also transferred to Auchterhouse Church. Almost 1300 years of worshipping in Tealing Church came to an end when the building closed.

The next minister of Murroes and Tealing Parish Church was the Rev. Helen Johnstone who was appointed on 28 September 1983 and made a bit of history as the first woman parish minister ever appointed by the Dundee Presbytery. At her instigation, the Tealing Kirk Heritage Centre was formed as a company limited by guarantee and successfully purchased the old church from the Church of Scotland. Rev. Johnstone and her fellow Directors, the Rev James A Roy and Mr Alan Grewar, had a vision of Tealing Church as a heritage Centre illustrating 1000 years of church life in a country parish.

Copious records and files from the ensuing years show that the Rev Johnstone and her husband, the Rev. Bob Johnstone, made strenuous efforts to make their vision reality. But it was not to be. They couldn't raise the significant amount of money required to fund the development and when, over the years, through ill-health, death and the moving away of the Directors, the company ceased to trade and was dissolved, ownership of Tealing Church finally reverted to the Crown in 1999. In the meantime, the church had become derelict and open to the elements. There was a real danger that its many relics and fine inscriptions would be permanently damaged. Last year, on behalf of the Crown, Angus Council made the building wind and watertight, at least halting the decay. Tealing Churchyard is still in use as a cemetery and is owned and administered by Angus Council.

Tealing Church 1958   *Courtesy of* D. C. *Thomson* & *Co. Ltd.*

16

PRESENT

Murroes and Tealing Church has been linked with Auchterhouse since February 1983. Many Tealing villagers still worship at the Murroes and Tealing Church and also at

Aucherhouse Church, where the joint Minister is now the Rev. Sydney Graham. Fittingly, the final words in this chapter are his" it was five years ago that a vacancy committee, comprising folk from Tealing, Murroes and Auchterhouse came to a church in Uplawmoor Renfrewshire, where I was preaching on Easterday. Bob Taylor was a good ambassador for Tealing that day! We met after the service in the borrowed Vestry, and then they had a meeting in the car park in a circle. It looked like an open-air service as we sneaked past, quietly.

Later that day they asked me to consider being your minister! Little did I know what adventures that would lead to. For nearly five years I have had the privilege of being your friend and minister. Sharing the joy, the laughter and perhaps too many times the tears of unexpected happenings in church, family and community life. We have laughed at weddings and shared hopes at baptisms, had our faith rocked but renewed at funerals. Love is stronger than death! We have worshiped together, socialised and gone on pilgrimage holidays together. Encouraged the school with pride. Started the Men's Regnal Circle. We have shared, with several student ministers our community talents and fears and hopes. A great privilege I don't deserve.

The high trees that surrounded the manse and the goat that greeted me when I came to reconnoitre have all gone. But for me green hills of the Sidlaws, have very much become the green hills of home! What a great heritage we have fallen heir to as newcomers, which most of us are, indebted to people in church and community who laid the foundations of community life here, who sowed seeds still coming to fruition. Creating true community is a costly business. Evolution depends on others improving what they inherit.

What kind of heritage is it we are leaving behind, from which others may spring forward? What balance of body mind and Spirit, in family and community life? We can't talk great dreams for the millennium; we have to live them now! There is a job for all of us in the synergy of community life. We too have to plough the fields and scatter the good seed on the land, or it will grow sour and unfruitful. Thanks for calling Edna and I here, and accepting us so well. I look forward to continue working with you as we build this community in the new millennium. What am I trying to say? Let's leave it to St. Paul 1 Thessalonians 2 -4" *We always thank God for you all and always mention you in our prayers. For we remember before God our Father how you put your faith into practice, how your love made you work so hard and how your hope in the Lord Jesus Christ is so firm. Our brothers and sisters we know that God loves you and has chosen you to be His own.*

17

CHAPTER 3 TEALING SCHOOLDAYS

EARLY HISTORY

In 1836, the Old Statistical Account for the Parish of Tealing reported "there are five schools in the parish, namely, 1 parochial school and four schools in detached situations, for comparatively young children. The parochial schoolmaster has the maximum salary, and his house and the schoolroom are in good condition. The general expense of education is so reasonable as to place it within the reach of almost all. The very few children, whose parents cannot afford to pay for their education, have their school fees paid from those funds, which are under the control of the session. All the inhabitants above six or eight years can read, and a great majority of them are qualified to write. The people in general are adequately alive to the benefits of education. There is one parochial library, which is regarded by the inhabitants with a lively interest, and is flourishing accordingly".

The writer, The Reverend David B Mellis, Minister of Tealing Parish Church, paints a positive picture. Education was not compulsory in 1836 and many children were not able to read and write. That Tealing supported five voluntary schools and the majority of its young children were literate is impressive and says much about their parents' commitment to the principle of education. Reverend Mellis does not say where these five schools were, but we know that the School House that sits alongside the current school was not built until around 1875. Angus Council Archives Unit has been unable to establish exactly when the current school was built, but the Old School House at Balgray may have been built as much as one hundred years earlier in the late 18th century. Whether these two sites were included in the Reverend's list is unclear and would require much further research.

COMPULSORY EDUCATION IN SCOTLAND

In 1872, the responsibility for education was transferred from churches to elected school boards, which provided compulsory education for children aged 5 to 13 years. The records of Tealing School Board meetings, from 1873 onwards, are a rich source of information about school times in the village.

At the first meeting of the School Board on 8 April 1873, it was reported that five members had been elected:

Mr Alexander Bell, Farmer, Balnuith, Tealing

Mr John Ogilvy, Factor, Hare Craig, Dundee

The Reverend Duncan Turner, Minister of the Free Church, Tealing

Mr William Ogilvie, Farmer, Newbigging, Tealing

Mr George Langlands, Farmer, Balkemback, Tealing

Mr Bell was elected Chairman of the Board and the Parochial Schoolmaster, Mr Alexander Menzies (the Dominie), was appointed Treasurer and Clerk. The Board had considerable powers and effectively ran all of the affairs of the school, including the appointment of staff, responsibility for the standard of education provided and all financial matters.

CENSUS OF EDUCATION **1873**

The Education (Scotland) Act of 1872 required that a census of education in the parish be undertaken. This was completed within a fortnight of the first School Board meeting and reported, on 26 April 1873, that there were 195 children in the parish (most families had five or more children), as follows:

aged 5 to 13 years and attending school	158
aged 3 to 13 years and not attending school	25
above the age of 13 years and attending school	12
Total	195

It was also reported that, at that time, there were three schools in the area:

The Parish, now, the Public	School Roll 105, In attendance 80
The Free Church School	Roll 34, In attendance 32
School at Balkello	Roll 25, In attendance 23

Between them, the three schools had accommodation for up to 210 pupils. The condition of the Public School and Free Church buildings was described as "good", Balkello being described as "indifferent".

THE TRANSFER OF THE FREE CHURCH SCHOOL

Just weeks later, in June 1873, the Minister of the Free Church, The Reverend Duncan Turner, asked for a special meeting of the Board to discuss his proposal that the Free Church School and School House be transferred to the Public School Board. The only conditions to be applied were that the present teacher be retained and that the Free Church congregation would have access to the schoolhouse periodically in the evenings and on Sundays. It would appear that the transfer was completed before the end of 1873. In November 1873, the Schoolmaster, Mr Alexander Menzies resigned as he had been appointed Rector of Webster's Seminary in Kirriemuir. It was agreed that the post be advertised at a salary of £60 per annum.

A period of uncertainty followed, with several unsatisfactory appointments, culminating on 28 September 1876 with a special meeting of the Board to consider" What is to be done with the Teachers". As a result, the Schoolmaster, Mr Forbes was dismissed with effect from the end of the year. On 2 January 1877, Mr Peter McKenzie was appointed Schoolmaster of "The First Public School". The records at this time indicate that the Board was still running two school buildings and they had begun calling them the "First" and "Second" Public Schools. The "First" most probably refers to the current school and the "Second" to the Old Free Church School at Balgray. By November of that year, the records indicate that the "Scotch" Education Department was putting the Board under pressure to close the Second Public School and it would appear that they did so, not long afterwards. The teacher at the second school, Miss Badenhead, was offered a teaching post at the surviving school providing she upgraded her teaching skills. She declined the offer and resigned in October 1877.

STABILITY AT LAST

Peter McKenzie became Schoolmaster at the tender age of 26, but appears to have brought about the stability, and improvement in standards, craved by the Board. The Board had, between 1874 and 1876 set about extending and improving the main school building and had also built a new schoolhouse, at a cost of £600. Mr McKenzie moved in and the records show that, by the time he completed the Tealing Census in 1891 (for the Schoolmaster was also the Registrar), his household comprised himself, his wife Bella, their five children aged between one and eleven years and their servant, seventeen year-old Barbara Lawson. Over the years the Board seems to have been frequently concerned about attendance. They appreciated the importance in a rural community of a

Schoolmaster McKenzie and pupils, 1905.

helping hand at harvest time, and school holidays were timed so that the children could help with the tattie picking, but beyond that, they were unrelenting. In 1880, they were poised to refer for prosecution local blacksmith, William Gibson, for employing a child who should have been at school. It seems to have done the trick and the boy returned. However, the records continue, through the decades, to meticulously record attendance levels, to a much greater degree than they record the educational development of the school.

THE SOUP KITCHEN SAGA

The great "Soup Kitchen Saga" of 1884 to 1888 is worth a mention for it appears to have caused a stooshie of gargantuan proportions. In 1884, all schools were asked by the Education Board to consider providing a soup lunch for the children. The Tealing School Board set about examining their options and tried to raise funds for the building of a kitchen, which they estimated would cost around £30 to £35 including equipment. They were delighted when Mr W S Fothringham Esq of Tealing House agreed to provide the kitchen and appointed his land steward, Mr Walter McNicoll, to work with the Board's architect. By the time the quotations came in the total cost had escalated to £118, but this appears to have been approved by the Board and Mr McNicoll. When this was reported back to Mr Fothringham he advised that he was only ever committed to funding £15 towards the cost of the kitchen, being under the impression that Lord Home was funding the other £15. Strong letters were exchanged and, in 1885,the building of the soup kitchen was cancelled amid much apparent consternation on both sides. Years later, the soup kitchen was finally opened in January 1888, after the Board had authorised the taking of an overdraft of £150.

RUNNING COSTS

In 1892, the General Accounts for the school showed:-

	£	s.	d.
Salary of Board Officers	8	-	-
Salary of Teachers	239	4	3
Incidentals	3	3	4
Books	1	19	9
Rent, taxes	6	9	4
Repairs	30	19	2
Fuel, light	10	16	-
Interest on Loan	24	16	-
Repayment of Principal	19	8	3
Interest on Bank Advance	2	2	2
Balance in Hand	17	15	9
	£364	14	-

In 1891, fees were abolished and state education became free throughout Scotland for children aged between five and fourteen years. In 1913, the Board advised the Department that there was no local demand for continuation classes (for those over the age of fourteen) and consequently, they had no intention of offering them. By February 1915, the number of children in the parish was down to 89, less than half the number recorded in 1873.

LOCAL EDUCATION AUTHORITIES TAKE OVER

In 1918, Local Education authorities were established to replace School Boards and the provision of secondary education was made mandatory. Thereafter, it is the school logbook, kept by the head teacher, from which we can glean information, albeit in much less detail. Health issues, rather than attendance seem to be of increasing concern. For example, in September 1921, it is recorded that two nurses examined all of the pupils "giving hints, especially to the girls, on the benefits of cleanliness" and later, that the nurse called to examine "two verminous children". In 1923, the log records that "many of the infants have been absent through illness or the want of boots on wet mornings". By contrast, that same year on April 26, some good cheer is reported when a holiday was observed in celebration of the marriage of the Duke of York to Elizabeth of Glamis.

In November 1926, with almost chilling detachment, it is reported that" a little boy in the Infant Department died on Wednesday evening from malignant scarlet fever. He was present in school on Tuesday. Attendance still very good, 92.10/0." In the following year another tragedy struck. A teacher, Miss Marshall, on her way home after school was involved in a motor collision and suffered severe head injuries. She died one week later on 8 December 1927.

On 28 April 1930, James McGregor took up duty as Headmaster, succeeding Dominie Dunn. In the following February he reports that" scholars in Junior and Senior Rooms have now been divided for each subject. Method is working satisfactorily and is an improvement on the old rigid Class Method".

WORLD WAR 11

War was declared on 3 September 1939 and the log reports that week, that the Headteacher, as Receiving Officer for children who were to be billeted in Tealing, met a party much smaller than expected 3 mothers, 5 pre-school children and 17 school children. Extra teaching staff was brought in to cope with the influx. School life seems to continue routinely throughout the war years although there are references to more evacuee children joining the school, to the air raid shelters, the giving out of Point Ration Books in the lunch breaks and to Mr Christie, the Science Teacher, being called to Military Service.

Mrs Elizabeth Hill had by now become the schools' first female Headteacher. In June 1944 the children were preparing posters for a competition during "Salute the Soldier" week. Saving Stamp prizes were presented to the winner at a concert in Tealing Hall. Later that month, with the opening of the attack on Western Europe, extra geography lessons were given to provide an elementary understanding of these great events. Padre Gillespie of the RAF also gave his monthly talk to the pupils.

On 7th May 1945, the school logbook records the "Beginning of a momentous week. The

22

pupils and staff are all excited awaiting the news of Germany's unconditional surrender. All classes have been preparing for VE DAY by learning allied and national songs and painting flags. Children subscribed to buy a flag for each classroom. At 3.00pm we heard the news of the German surrender as broadcast by the Germans, but no announcement from S.H.A.E.F. Bonfire prepared in playground and flags hoisted. Before closing whole school assembled and sang "Land of Our Birth" and" God Save the King". Three cheers were given for the Army, the Navy and the Air Force.

On 8 May, "at 3.00pm Mr Churchill broadcast the official announcement of Unconditional Surrender by Germany. VE DAY".

On 11May, "school re-opened after VE DAY holidays. Children told of their experiences and the surrender and its significance was discussed. A large percentage of the children had attended the Thanksgiving Service and Party on VE evening. The local hall was decorated with flags and slogans coloured by the schoolchildren. Bonfire in the playground and children danced around it singing".

THE FIFTIES AND SIXTIES

Mr Maurice McLean came to Tealing Primary School in 1952. He recalls "When I first went to Tealing the school and the schoolhouse were or more or less unchanged from the 1930's. The headmaster had always been known as the Dominie and I inherited that title. We had two classrooms, Miss Hendry taught P1, 2, 3 and sometimes 4 and I taught P5, 6, 7 and sometimes 4. A smaller back room was used for dining and a dinner at that time cost 6 old pence, two course lunch, no choice of menu, take it or leave it. Water came from a hillside spring filled tank across the field behind the school. Each room had a coal fire. In snowstorms, meals often couldn't be brought from Forfar. Pupils who could make it each brought a bread and butter sandwich. Each country school had emergency rations some tins of corned beef, cocoa and powdered milk. We boiled water on the classroom fire and made cocoa to drink and corned beef sandwiches to eat.

Each room had a paraffin lamp hanging in the middle of the ceiling. The floor under each lamp had a big oily stain where drips had fallen for years. The toilets were outside. Girls on the west side, boys behind the school where later a nice dining hall was built. In the mid-fifties, when mains water and electricity came to the village we got indoor toilets, electric lights and fan heaters. School-garden education for the boys stopped in 1948 but the boys remembered it and, in my first year, some of them offered to help me plant most of the back garden with potatoes to clean it. When they made beautiful drills for the planting, I was charmed to see, like true farmers, they had made "end-rigs" at the top and bottom of the plot.

At first we had an old battery-set wireless in my room for P4 -7. Later, I got an old mains set from a parent and, from another old set, took the speaker and invented an extension to the infant's room. We had no television in my time at the school. The assistant and I did

23

our own PE in the classroom or outside. We also taught music although the wireless was a great help for teaching songs with professional accompaniment. Each year we had very successful sports and a fund -raising whist drive. As Dominie I was given the job of Superintendent of Tealing Graveyard. Mrs McLean usually took the undertaker's phone calls. After a funeral, he often came to me at the school to settle the account. Most pupils progressed to their first year at the Murroes expect for those who were successful in the "Control Exam". They went on to Forfar Academy. Their future at this time greatly concerned parents and me".

CENTENARY CELEBRATION

In June 1972, in common with other schools throughout Scotland, Tealing Primary School celebrated 100 years of compulsory schooling. The teaching team at this time consisted of the Headteacher Mr Sturrock, Mrs Eisler, Miss Fraser and Miss Brown and, with the children, they set about building an exhibition of the school in Victorian times. What started as a school project became a mass village effort as villagers raided their attics for old-time mementoes. Old photographs, paintings, Victorian furniture, clothes, toys, books and knick-knacks were laid out in the school. Miss Fraser dressed up as an old Victorian school ma' am and many of the children wore the long white pinnies, frilled bonnets and black boots of the era. Parents and friends came along to view the exhibition, sat down to coffee and sandwiches and heard a programme of songs from the children, arranged by Mrs Sturrock.

Mr Sturrock composed a special school song for the occasion:

TEALING SCHOOL SONG.

(To the tune Villikins and Dinah. The spirit of William McGonagall lives on!)

On the slopes of the Sidlaws
'N eath bonnie Craigoul,
In the parish of Tealing
There stands a wee school.

Nearby flows the Fithie
On its way to the sea
In the heart of the country
Yet near to Dundee.

'Twas built in the year
Eighteen Seventy Two-
For an act passed by Parliament
Said, "This you must do!

24

All you parents of children
Aged five to thirteen,
To school you must send them!
Signed -Victoria the Queen.

The Dominie and Missie
Will patiently try
To pass on their learning
Until by-and-by,
Each child in the school-room
Is reasonable slick
At reading and writing
And A-rith-me-tic!

1972

All of this was reported in the local newspaper "The People's Journal" on 3 June 1972. A full page of coverage and photographs was included, providing a marvellous record for the school archives. More importantly, it had been tremendous fun for everyone involved.

PERSONAL MEMORIES

To get even more of a flavour of what it was like to attend Tealing Primary School we asked some ex-pupils (aged between 18 and 88) and one current pupil, to share their memories. The result is a series of vivid recollections that capture the rate of change over the years and portray some very happy times.

MRS JANET KIRKBY

I was born at Hillside, Tealing in March 1912. My father, Adam Key, had to go over the Sidlaw hills on horseback to Glamis for the doctor -no telephones or cars in those days! When I became a pupil at Tealing Public School in 1917, I joined my sister Agnes who was two years my senior. The teacher was Miss Thomson and Dominie Dunn was the headmaster, who was also the Registrar of births and deaths. Eleven pupils from Hillside attended the school, six from the Patterson family, three from the Chalmers family (my cousins) and two Keys. Together we were known as "The Hillsiders".

There was a soup kitchen run by Miss Marr and we all took our own sandwiches, not in boxes like today! The toilets at the back of the school were not the "flushing type" and certainly not hygienic by today's standards. Mr Dunn was owner of one of the first cars in the district, a Ford named the "Tin Lizzie"! During school hours when he was driving the car we ran to meet him to get a hurl in this modern contraption. Slate and slate pencils were the main mode of writing, but we did possess one jotter in which we could write an essay. Heating was from two large open coal fires, one in each room.

In 1921, we all attended the Dedication Service for the War Memorial. It was a memorable day and we sang the hymns we had rehearsed at school beforehand, "Now Israel May Say" and "How Bright Those Glorious Spirits Shine". If the weather was inclement, which was often, the horse and cart from the farm transported the children through the deep snow. In March in the lambing season, my father and the shepherd spent many a night tending the sheep and their lambs. Pet lambs were often in the kitchen being fed from a bottle. There was no electricity or gas, so heating and lighting came from coal fires and paraffin lamps. After I passed my 11+ exam and gained a Carnegie Bursary, I went to the Morgan Academy in Dundee, cycling the seven miles each way in all types of weather.

(Mrs Kirkby is now retired and lives in North Berwick. She retains a fondness for Tealing Kirk as she was married there in 1939. She recently came back to Tealing Primary School, accompanied by the Rev. Sydney Graham, to share her memories with today's pupils, a visit she found "most enjoyable").

JANET (McLELLAN) STEWART

I attended Tealing Primary School from August 1944, aged five, until 1951 when I left, aged twelve. The head teacher was Mrs Elizabeth Hill who taught primaries five, six and seven. Primaries one to four were taught by Miss Cant. The number of children varied during the year, when their fathers took a "fee" to work on another farm or in another parish. In the same way, new children regularly came in to the school from outside the parish. The number of children in each primary was usually five or six.

Our daily routine was the same throughout the year, but in the summer days we were allowed outdoors in the playing field for drawing and nature study lessons. Most of the children had school dinners, which were cooked in the school kitchen by Mrs McKay and served in the dining hall, a wooden building which still exists today. We were also given a small bottle of milk to drink each day. My long-held memory of the school is of the huge coal fire in the big classroom, surrounded by frozen bottles of milk thawing and of the smell of wet woollen gloves drying by the fire.

(Janet went on to work in a day nursery and then left to train as an enrolled nurse. She still lives in the village with her husband Fred).

LINDSAY HAY

My mum, dad and uncle were all at Tealing School in the 1920's and 1930's. Tealing was still part of the Fothringham Estate, for whom my grand ad worked. My brothers and I attended Tealing Primary School between 1955 and 1969. The Dominie was Mr McLean and the teachers at that time were Mrs Cook and Mrs Harberton. When Mr Mclean left, Mr Sturrock took over. The teachers then were Mrs Eisler and Miss Fraser.

We walked to school, whereas today most children get on the bus. The sports day just before going on holiday was what everyone looked forward to. There were outings but not everyone could afford to go. The holidays were working holidays, berry picking in the summer and potato picking in the autumn. All the money made was spent on clothes for the school. The summers were a lot better then, not so much rain, but winter was from November through to March. There could be snow on the ground for all of that time, not now.

We didn't have goal posts at first but we got them made and started a football team. Now the school entrance is at the side but it used to be at the front. My job was to ring the school bell after playtime. There were three classrooms -primaries 1 and 2, primaries 3 and 4 and then the big classroom. We didn't have to walk far to end our school year, just down to Tealing Church, which is no longer in use.

(Lindsay still lives in the family cottage in Tealing. He is a keen gardener and is often seen out and about cycling around the country lanes).

SHONA CAMPBELL

(with input from younger sisters Kirsteen and Ailsa)

I attended Tealing Primary School from 1981 to 1988. When I started I was in Mrs Kohler's class and the school had 50 pupils. By the time I reached primary five, the fall in numbers meant that Tealing had become a two-teacher school and Mr Sturrock taught me for my last three years. By 1988, there were only 33 pupils.

I remember the school getting its first computer, a BBC (I don't actually remember ever using it!), the inter-school sports days with Auchterhouse and Strathmartine, school ski trips to Braemar, and the tuck shop "pickled onion space invaders and a cola quenchy cup please". In 1988, to celebrate Dundee's 800th anniversary, we had a year long project on Dundee. The masterpiece being a mural/collage the length of the library wall that took weeks to do, a postcard picture of Dundee from Tayport, everyone adopting their own landmark (I was lucky enough to get the big gas cylinder!). There was the garden path between the school and the School House that we had to look after. A proud moment for all of us was when we won the Dolphin Trophy, two years running for the most swimming badges earned per head in Scotland (or was it Dundee?).

In the autumn we would build leaf barricades in the narrow passage at the back of the dining hall. We would run and jump then build a bit higher. In the summer we played handstands in the pitch to the cry of "Forks, Knives and Carrots", would make potions at the witchy tree or play housies at the housie tree. In the winter we would play on icy slides (my rubber soles were never the best), roll snowmen and burrow tunnels in the heaps of snow left at the side of the playground by the snowploughs. When it rained we would congregate in the Sheddies. We would play "a fast train to ...." I used to watch in rapture as the older kids swung on the rafters, then when I was a big primary 7; it was my turn to show off. It is the playground that my most vivid memories revolve around.

(Shona went on to university and is now an accountant with Deloitte in Glasgow. Her sisters are both at university).

TOM STRANG

In August 1993 I started at Tealing School and I am now in Primary 7. My teacher from Primaries 1-4 was Mrs Chidley, who is still teaching this stage. Since Primary 5 My main teacher has been Miss Hendry, the headteacher, but we have other teachers too, especially Mrs Wright and Mrs Wilkie. Teachers for P.E., Art and Music also visit the school and the older children get swimming lessons each year. In August last year a morning nursery class taught by Mrs Willison started.

Every year we have special events. In October we have a fancy dress Halloween party and in December we practise carols, readings and a nativity play for the Christmas service. In the Spring term most of the pupils learn a Scottish poem and the Primary 7 pupils can enter the Leng Medal competition. In recent years we have also entered the Soccer Sevens tournament. In the Summer term every year we have a sports afternoon and we also go on a school trip. Some of the places we have been to include the Sea Life Centre, Praytis Farm Park, Camperdown Park and the Scottish Deer Centre.

Last year the older children took part in "Opera for All" and this year it will be the ecological musical "Yanomamo". After the Summer holidays I shall be starting at Forfar Academy and I hope that I'll like it as much as Tealing.

(Tom lives with his parents Eileen and Alexander Strang and sister Alison at Balcalk Farm, Tealing)

TEALING PRIMARY SCHOOL, 2000

Today, the school remains at the heart of village life. The parents, friends and relatives of the 40 children currently at the school, as generations have done before, delight in supporting school events, anniversaries and celebrations. And the school continues to provide a focus for the future for everyone in the village. It is therefore fitting, in this millennium year, that the final words in this chapter come from Miss Linda Hendry, Headteacher of Tealing Primary School:

"I started at Tealing School in August 1988 -there were 27 children on the roll. During my time we have had the establishment of a very active P.T.A. and School board: the opening of Tealing Nursery and the introduction of a school uniform, chosen and designed by pupils. Probably the most important development has been the introduction of computers so that all pupils have computer access, and can use the computers confidently to enhance their learning.

The children participate in too many activities to list here. They have won many awards both nationally and locally. The school is particularly keen to develop in the children appreciation and care of their environment. Around the school they have planted trees, established gardens and planted many bulbs which are very lovely at this time. We encourage pupils to play a positive role within the community, we encourage links with older residents and have had former pupils of many years ago, talking to the children of their experiences; the pupils have entertained residents and they are invited to various school activities. The pupils take part in fund raising for many charities.

It is said that "Children are our Future". The future of Tealing School and the surrounding area seems to be very promising indeed."

Tealing Primary School Children and Staff, April 2000.

29

CHAPTER 4
PROMINENT PEOPLE

In any area there will be people who are well known and well remembered. This may be because they were eminent in their chosen fields, because they made a particular contribution or because they were real characters and were simply unforgettable. Throughout this story of Tealing, many individuals are mentioned in the course of covering a specific part of Tealing's history. This chapter gives more detailed information on those who, for various reasons, made a particular impression.

WALTER McNICOLL

THE TEALING GEOLOGIST

1827-1908

Walter McNicoll was a native of the Kirriemuir district and came to Tealing in 1850, at the age of 23 years, to work on the Fothringham Estate. For forty years he was in the service of Mrs Fothringham of Tealing and her grandson Mr W S Fothringham, becoming Land Steward and Manager of Tealing Home Farm. He was also an eminent geologist, agriculturalist and botanist. It was said that no one knew the geology of the Sidlaws better than he and he had a reputation especially in connection with red sandstone and its fossils. Throughout his life he roamed the Angus countryside making explorations and searching for fossils. He kept meticulous records of his finds, regularly submitting evidence for publication in papers for the Society of Antiquaries of Scotland.

It is largely as a result of his work that Tealing's ancient stones and landmarks have been recorded and it was under his supervision that Tealing Earth-house was excavated in 1871. Many of the fossils and specimens he collected were very valuable and have ended up in the museums of Dundee and Edinburgh. He lived in Tealing for 58 years and was a loyal United Free Churchman, an elder of the Tealing Free Church for 25 years.

During his lifetime, some of his specimens were figured and described by Professor Huxley and Mr Salter on Monograph I, published by the Geological Survey of the United Kingdom, who thanked him for his "zeal and liberality". When he died in July

1908, the Reverend Neil Elder also described him as "universally respected, unostentatious, retiring and a man who walked humbly with his God."

James L Purgavie
The Tealing Poet
1859-Unknown

James Lindsay Purgavie came to Tealing in 1885, at the age of 26 years, to take up the position of Gamekeeper on the Estate of Mr Fothringham of Fothringham. He began to rhyme partly to pass the time, and partly for amusement, and often spent the night on the hillside watching for some unwary member of the poaching fraternity. And so he started trying to relieve the tedium of watching and waiting by putting some of his thoughts and experiences into verse. His work became well known locally, leading in March 1900, by the request of many, to the publication of his book of poetry "Hillside Musings" printed by James P Mathew of Cowgate, Dundee, with a preface by the Reverend S Macaulay, Minister of Tealing Parish Church. Rev. Macaulay described James Purgavie as "a married man not unacquainted with the way of bairns" and said that he
"describes nature as he has seen her and life as he has found it."

Doon by the Burn

Doon by the burn I tak' a turn
In summer for a troot
It's braw to stare and see them there
Aye jinkin' in and oot

The sport is fine wi' rod an' line
An' hooks, an bait, an' reel
When burnie broon comes tum'lin doon
Oh, then to fill the creel!

A big hill shoo' er, a heavy poor
A burnie doon in spate
A red worm lure, the troots are sure
To mouth the temptin' bait

(there are a further nine verses and then it ends as follows)

It comes at will, an' strange the thrill
When fresh life-thochts are given
Doon by the burn I tak' a turn
An' earth ay seems like heaven

James Lindsay Purgavie

SIR STEWART DUKE-ELDER

1898-1978

Stewart Duke-Elder was born in Tealing on 22 April 1898, son of the Tealing Free Church Minister, the Reverend Neil Elder. He graduated MA (Hons) in Natural Science and BSc with distinction in physiology. He qualified in 1923, obtained the FRCS in 1924 and proceeded MD in 1925 and became an eminent ophthalmologist. In 1932 he operated on the then Prime Minister, Ramsay Macdonald for glaucoma. At an early age he was appointed surgeon oculist to King Edward VIII and subsequently to King George VI and then to Queen Elizabeth 11.He was knighted in 1933.

He was also known for his many contributions to medical literature, publishing the System of Ophthalmology, in fifteen volumes, the first being published in 1958 and the last in 1976. Early in life he learnt to depend on fewer hours of sleep than most people need and that is part of the reason for his most amazing output of learned papers and books throughout his life. In World War 11,he was consultant ophthalmic surgeon to the Army with the rank of Brigadier. He was made an honorary member of practically all the ophthalmologic societies in the world and of many other scientific bodies, and was given numerous honorary degrees and fellowships.

His obituary in the British Medical Journal further described him as "a warm-hearted and friendly Scot, with his charming smile and puckish sense of humour he would at once put strangers at their ease." Sir Stewart Duke-Elder died on 27 March 1978 aged 79 and was survived by his wife Phyllis Duke-Elder.

COUNCILLOR GEORGE MUDIE
1899-1968

George Mudie represented Murroes & Tealing on Angus Council from 1945 until 1968. He had a keen interest and affection for Tealing and was instrumental in having the council houses built at Inveraldie. He served on a number of committees, but his greatest interests were in education and housing.

As a young man he lived in the farmhouse at Whitehouse which his parents rented until May 1924, when the grandparents of the present Nicoll family took over the property. In 1932 he moved to the Newbigging Road. He was very active in the community, highly regarded and well respected. During his stewardship of the area he staunchly represented the interests of Tealing at Angus County Council and with many others. It is widely believed that the Dalziel place names in Inveraldie are so called after his wife's maiden name.

DAVIE GLEN

1909-1978

Without doubt, the name mentioned the most often, when talking about Tealing "characters", is that of Davie Glen. Twenty-two years after his death he is still fondly and vividly remembered by many local people. Davie, in over 45 years of climbing, "diddling" and story telling, became one of the best-known and most popular characters in Angus. Nor was his fame confined to his home county. For his weather-beaten features, complete with beard were seen on virtually every mountain on the mainland of Scotland -and at the ceilidhs, which go hand-in-hand with climbing.

Davie Glen.

Davie lived in a converted railway carriage in School Road Tealing for more than thirty years and it became almost as well known as the hostels, lodges and bothies frequented by the climbing fraternity. All of his life he was the outdoor type. In 1972, in an interview for the Evening Telegraph, he said "I started cycle racing in 1927. During the Thirties I turned semi-professional, going round the games and sports in the area. I made a copper or two to ease the burden during the Depression. I remember one day I stopped at a wee shop in Forfar for a bottle of lemonade. The woman there asked me if I had been cycling fast. I replied that I had been going so hard that the telegraph poles flashed by like the teeth of a comb!" At that point, Davie added that out of 112 lie-telling competitions he has entered, he had won 104. "That's the kind of thing I would tell" he grinned. At that time "pass storming" was very popular with cyclists. "I remember one Sunday in 1930 when I made a round trip of about 130 miles" Davie continued. "I left Westhall Terrace, Duntrune at 5.30 a.m., cycled to Braemar without stopping and had a snack there. Then I went on through Glen Tilt, carrying the bike for about seven miles, and had another snack at Forest Lodge. From there I made for Dunkeld, where I met up with some of the lads out for their Sunday run. After having a drum-up together we cycled to Perth and then had our usual race into Dundee, arriving about 9.30 p.m."

He had stopped cycling in 1967. "A blackbird built a nest in the front wheel," he said, pointing to an old bike at the end of the carriage, "and I didn't want to disturb it." The first mountain he climbed was Beinn a' Beithir, south of Fort William, in 1931 when he was

33

working on the road building. "The name means Ben of the Thunderbolt. I'd heard shepherds say that if mountains groaned bad weather would follow. "The day I climbed Beinn a Beithir I heard it groaning. It's an eerie sound, sort of like two grindstones rubbing together. "Sure enough, for the next three days the rain bucketed down." On Christmas Eve, 1935, he almost died from exhaustion and exposure on Bidean nam Bean, in Glencoe. "I tackled too much and had to find my way off the mountain in the dark in terrible conditions. "By the time I got down my ice-axe was frozen to my glove in a solid block of ice. It was only sheer will power that got me to safety."

When the war came, Davie was working on a hydro tunnel in Glen Tromie. The day France fell in 1940, he decided to join up after a short holiday. A few nights later found him at the hostel in Glen Nevis. He suggested to his fellow visitors that they should climb the Ben and watch the sunrise. More than 20 enjoyed what Davie referred to as one of his most wonderful experiences. A friend who was later lost at sea suggested that after the war they should organise an annual sunrise expedition. From this suggestion came the Lochnagar Sunrise Expedition in 1949. Over 700 people joined in. Davie went on all of the Lochnagar Expeditions until 1969.

After Ben Nevis, Davie joined the RAF. Two years later he was in civvies again, due to an ulcer and a spinal complaint. "A lot of concerts were being held to raise money for the war effort so I started going in for the diddling competitions. "They were always lie telling a competition at these affairs and this was what I liked best. "Diddling is fairly easy compared with making up stories. You can learn a tune from a record and diddle to it, but a story is something that you have to make up yourself." Davie twice won the National Diddling Championship. His proficiency led to several TV appearances, the first being on the Wilfred Pickles Show, in London. It was his one and only trip to the capital. "The best thing about that place was the Flying Scotsman coming back home," he said.

Davie led thousands of people on hill treks, taking a bus party almost every month. A number of accidents occurred during his climbing career. In 1966 he built a bothy four miles from Glen Doll, near the place where four Glasgow hikers perished in 1959. He used stones from the ruin of a hut, but still had to trek from Glen Doll with timber for the roof. The Forfar & District Hill Walking Club helped to carry up the corrugated iron for the roof. Davie worked at tree-planting, draining, tunnelling, drystane dyking and roadwork.

In 1972, he had decided to leave his native Angus and retire to Inverness-shire. "The sea mists in this area are not suitable for bronchitis," he said. However, he stayed for only a few months and soon he was back home in his railway carriage in Tealing. In April 1978, Davie was found lying unconscious in heavy rain one morning, just outside the railway carriage, by his neighbours Martin and Linda Scott. They called for an ambulance and summoned help from their neighbours Fred and Janet Stewart. Davie was taken to Ninewells Hospital where he died shortly afterwards, his place in Scottish folklore preserved forever.

There is a man whose weel kent face
Stands out in every crowd
His kilted form, his long grey beard
His voice still clear and loud

At ceilidhs he's the brightest light
He aye comes back again
I hope for many years ahead
We'll hear "o" Davie Glen

Let other Scotsmen rise and fall
They may be honest men
But brightly gleams abune them "a"
The name "o" Davie Glen!

Best wishes from Jean Spence "wha's doorstep in Dundee you once sat on, gie cauld!"

DR LAWRENCE EDWARD LUSCOMBE
RETIRED BISHOP OF BRECHIN

For twelve years now, Dr L E Luscombe, Retired Bishop of Brechin, better known throughout Scotland to his friends, family and church colleagues as "Ted", has lived in the village of Tealing. This came about in 1988, when protracted ill health resulted in the amputation of his wife Doris's right leg below the knee and a house on one level was urgently needed. Ted found the bungalow at Kirkton of Tealing quite quickly and recalls realising right away that it was an ideal location for their approaching retirement. "Woodville" also served as his official residence for the final year of his episcopate as Bishop of Brechin and Primus of the Scottish Episcopal Church.

Lawrence Edward Luscombe was born on 10 November 1924 in Torquay. In November 1942 he joined the army and completed his training as a private soldier in the Border Regimental Depot at Carlisle Castle. There it was decided that he was" officer material" and he was sent to India to join the Officer Training School at Bangalore. He then served in Assam, the jungle of North West Burma and the Indian Sapper Depot in Jullundur in the Punjab, where he later became Acting Major. During his time at Jullundur, Ted met and married Doris, a young doctor from Glasgow who had almost certainly saved his life when she treated him for malaria and amoebic dysentery. They returned to the UK in 1947 when Lord Mountbatten handed over his powers as Viceroy to the new Indian Government.

Ted decided on an accountancy career and became a partner with Galbraith, Dunlop and Co, qualifying as a Chartered Accountant in 1952. He remained a very active member of the church and, in 1960, felt a strong calling to the ordained ministry. What followed was an outstanding achievement for one who did not start training for the ministry until he was 36 years old. After years of study, Ted was ordained Deacon in St Mary's Episcopal Cathedral Glasgow in September 1963 and to the priesthood, also in Glasgow Cathedral, in May 1964. He went on to become Provost of St Paul's Cathedral Dundee in 1971, Bishop of Brechin in June 1975 and Primus of the Scottish Episcopal Church in 1985, before retiring in January 1990.

Throughout his period in the church, and to this day, he has given sterling service to many committees and other organisations including Aberlour Children's Trust, Dr Barnardo's, the Slessor Centre Trust and, in the field of education, at Glenalmond, Lathallan and Northern College. In 1987, the University of Dundee conferred upon him the Degree of Doctor of Laws honoris causa. Since then he has completed a Master of Philosopy and PhD, becoming an Honorary Research Fellow at the University of Dundee. Typically, soon after arriving in Tealing he began to make a contribution to village life, serving on the Hall Committee and the School Board, of which he is still a member. Sadly, Doris died four years after coming to live in Tealing, but Ted has stayed on and continues to enjoy a very active retirement.

Over the years there have been many tributes to Bishop Luscombe. Just before his retirement, his life and career were recorded in the book "Edward; Reminiscences and Recollections" published in 1989 by Burns & Harris Ltd. A fuller biography is currently being written by John S Peart-Binns and will be published in the near future. Looking back on his career, a fellow Bishop said about him "by gentle persuasion and patient explanation he has steered, worked and captained the ship safely and confidently. It has all been done by a happy mix of serpent's wisdom and the dove's perceptive innocence. Ted is a man of stature. But to his great ability is added genuine humility, a warm humanity and overflowing generosity."

Tealing, the Road to the Sidlaws.

CHAPTER 5 18TH & 19TH CENTURY COMMUNITY LIFE

EARLY HISTORY

Tealing is firmly a rural community. Hundreds of years ago the six or so miles between Tealing and Dundee or Forfar must have seemed like distance enough to place the city and the toon "far, far away". In such times, the village of Tealing, like many other places, was much more self-sufficient, producing crops and milk for consumption, as well as for sale. Life then centred around the land, the church and each other, making tight knit communities where" abody kent abody else". Large families with more than 10 children were not uncommon and kith and kin often remained in the one area for generations. Life was at times hard and uncompromising, but there was a very strong sense of community.

Writing in 1790, the Rev. John Gellatly reported for the Statistical Account that the population of Tealing had risen from 735 to 802 (made up of 158 families). He attributed the increase to the erection of some new farms and said "several young people move southward to learn the handicraft trades. The annual average of births is 23, marriages 6, of burials 18. A woman about twenty years ago died here at the age of 102. The number of considerable farmers is 13. Besides these there may be 15 or 16 who possess from 10 to 30 acres each, and 1 or 2 horses. The other great class of inhabitants is weavers, of which there are about 90 employed in the manufacture of coarse linens, which find a ready market at Dundee. The flax is mostly foreign and brought from the town just mentioned, but the far greater part of the yarn is spun in the parish".

Farming life was well covered in this account. He added "the number of horses is about 200. Black cattle being used in labour now, there are about 30 kept for that purpose, cows about 300. With regard to sheep it is remarkable that about 25 years ago there were 12 small flocks in the parish, but now there is not a single animal of the kind, save a few kept by a gentleman for the use of his own family. They were found destructive to the sown grass and liable to perish for want of proper shelter. Young black cattle have been, with great advantage, put in their place. The number of acres is about 3000. The parish does more than supply itself with the articles of oatmeal, barley, beef, ale, whisky and potatoes. It sends to Dundee and other places,

Barley, 900 bolls at 13s and 4d	£600
Oatmeal, 500 bolls at 13s and 4d	£330
Calves for the butchers, 150	£100
Coarse linens to the value of	£4000
Black cattle, 200	£1400
Hay, 10,000 stone	£330
Whisky	£200
Milk, butter, cheese	£500
Total	£7460

The people always sow as soon as the season and the condition of the land permit. It must however be owned that they reap later than some of their neighbours. Harvest commonly begins about the 10th September. There are about 280 acres in wood, arable enclosed 550.The land rent is about £1400". On the issue of labour he added" as a child in this part of the country commonly finds employment at 8 or nine years of age, a labourer has seldom, entirely at least, upon his hands more than 3 children at once, that number he brings up without assistance. If they are all well, his wife, besides taking care of her family, may earn a shilling a week by spinning, nay, provided they have a cow, which is generally the case, they may earn another two shillings in the same space by the sale of butter for three months in the year. The wages of a good plough man, in general, are from £8 to £9 sterling annually, those of a maid servant, including her bounties as they are called, £3."

He described the people of Tealing as being "in general, of middle size. The condition of the people for the most part, is rather more than tolerable, and they are apparently contented with it. It might be better in some measure by making their cottages more comfortable and convenient, by raising better fences round their gardens and introducing the culture of a few more nourishing vegetables. The people have much improved in dress and manners. Among the men, instead of the bonnet and coarse home made woollens, the hat, English cloth and cotton stuffs are much worn, and almost every ploughman has his silver watch. The women still retain the plaid, but among the better sort it is now sometimes of silk or lined with silk, and numbers of them, on occasions, dress in ribbons, printed cottons, white stockings and lasted shoes.

The labouring servants, formerly ignorant and lazy, are now skilful and laborious. The farmers live in much more sociable manner and entertain with great hospitality. Their houses, formerly covered with thatch are now generally slated and contain 2 floors. As Mr Scrymsoure of Tealing resides on the spot, his improvements have been extensive. He has within these thirty years, planted 260 acres of moor-ground with trees of different kinds; among which are a thousand larches; enclosed and properly sub-divided upwards of 300 acres of arable with good stone fences, and near 100 acre of pasture and meadow ground, erected 3 considerable new farms and let a number of convenient possessions to the manufacturers at very reasonable rents upon the whole. He keeps a considerable farm in his own hand, and excites his tenants to the practice of good husbandry by his own example."

This remarkable account of Tealing in 1790 portrays an industrious place where families could find plenty of work and live reasonably well. However, writing a postscript in 1792, the Rev. Gellatly reported that there had been a sudden increase in deaths in the parish, which he attributed to "epidemical sore throat". He was deeply troubled by it and took the view that many of the deaths could have been avoided if only proper medical assistance had been available.

THE SECOND STATISTICAL ACCOUNT

Just less than fifty years later in 1836, the Rev David B Mellis's account of the parish was less detailed than the earlier one, but was nevertheless informative. He reported that the population had fluctuated;

1811	779
1821	725
1831	766

and he put the decrease from 1790 down to the enlarging of farms and the tendency for manufacturing jobs in the cities to attract villagers. The annual average of births was 17, marriages 5, of burials 8 -down on all counts. 3670 acres of land were either cultivated or occasionally in tillage and the average rent of arable land per acre was £1 and 15 shillings. Grazing a cow or ox cost £3 for the year. A common country labourer earned 10 shillings a week in the summer and 9 shillings weekly in the winter. He added " there are about thirteen thrashing machines in the parish, driven by water. As to cropping, the prevailing mode is to subject anyone field to the following rotation: green crop, barley with grass, hay crop, pasture, and afterwards oats. The distance from Dundee being only five or six miles, a ready and eligible market is obtained for all kinds of agricultural produce and, on the other hand, the transportation of manure from the town to the country is carried on to great extent. The general duration of leases is nineteen years. There are some quarries in the parish, from which a good deal of pavement is extracted and conveyed to Dundee". The value of sales from the quarries in 1836 was £200 per annum.

The total value of produce and manufacture had increased to £17,565 per annum, but whisky and coarse linen had disappeared from the list of produce reported in 1790. Intriguingly, Rev. Mellis stated" there are in the parish one inn and two ale-houses, but they do not appear to have produced, to any considerable extent, a deteriorating effect on the morals of the people".

During the 16th and 17th centuries several prominent families had obtained interests in portions of the Barony of Tealing -including the Ogilvys, the Lords Boyd, the Campbells of Lundie, Kinnaird of Clochindarge, the Grahams of Claverhouse (later called Lord Douglas) and the Earl of Strathmore. But from the early 1400s until the early 1700s the Maxwells of Tealing dominated. However, in 1836, the Rev Mellis reported that "the family of Mr Scrymseour (later to be known as the Fothringham Scrymseours) is the only one of influence or importance resident in the parish".

40

TURN OF THE CENTURY

As reported more fully in Chapters 2 and 3, throughout the 19th century, change was taking place in the church and in the schools apace. When the Rev. B Mellis and the majority of his congregation "came out" to form the Tealing Free Church in 1843, local people must have experienced great upheaval. Children would have been moved from parish and farm schools to the Free Church School. There may have been tension between those who moved on and those few who remained in the congregation of Tealing Parish Church. At the very least, such momentous events would have been the source of much discussion, debate and concentration. In 1872, compulsory education was introduced for all children aged between 5 and 13 years, changing the shape of the workforce and limiting the availability of children to work on the land. Farmers were concerned that production would be affected and lobbied on the timing of the school holidays to ensure the availability of child labour for harvesting.

Mrs Eisler, a former teacher at Tealing Primary School, provided the following poem. Written by H Lamont, it tells of the grand day had by all at the Tealing Bazaar in 1909 and provides a revealing and entertaining snapshot of community life at the time.

HIGH JINKS AT TEALING

Hae ye heard O' the doings we're haeing at Tealin'?
Maun it beats a, does the way we're a feeling
The pressure O' folk wha've come frae near & afar
Tae buy a' the goods frae the Tealin' Bazaar.

The schule, superintended by dominie Dunn,
For the nonce was gie'd o'er tae a kinds o'fun;
Frae the moment 'twis opened by Mrs Hay Morray,
Folk frae Nor', South, East, West earn' a' in a hurry.

The stalls gaily deck'd by one Mr Martin
Were fu at the time the proceedings were startin'
But, losh, by the time the day was weel o'er,
O' articles left there scarce was a score

What was sold, to recount would tak' mony weeks,
For great and for sma' o'baith sexes, were breeks,
While semmits for fat and for lean hung the wa',
Wi" socks O' a fits for great and for sma'.

41

Of cheer for the stammak there was a gran' stock
O' Gibson's lam'd candy and sweeties an rock,
There was tea and besides other known tee-tee-drinks,
But a few had a dram in their pouches methinks,

Ma certes the air wi the music was fu',
An a saxpence to heart I for ane didna' rue',
The pianny was hammer'd by Florrie and Mabel
We' a phonograph rival on David Fife's table.

There were songs new and auld at the beck o'Miss Slidders
But Jane Anne's "Auld Hoose" knock'd them a; into smidders
There's ane Mrs Miller wha'd walk'd five lang miles,
Tae quash the precentor who came up with a smile,

While the row that was raised 'ONE only could quell,
He's kent a aboot by the name Willy Bell,
A douce gentle, godfearin' elder is he
As only aboot the broad Mearns ye would see

Just the lad that I warrant will see things a richt
In the kirk where he stan's as a bricht shining licht;
An he disna mind greetin' his leader in prayer
When they dinna quite hit it wi' just a wee swear.

But eneuch 0 sic clatter, the part to entrance
Was the jig and the reels O; the threepenny dance;
Wi' skirl and wi' screech and fine hieland frenzy
Excitement rose high when oot stepp'd McKenzie.

There, danc'd Keay O'Newmains and Mrs McLeod
David Taylor wha helped wi' the phonograph loud,
Mrs Martin and spouse and parson Macaulay
footed it oot o'er the floor gay and brawly

But nicht maun draw on and day licht maun flee,
Say the mony guid wishes frae bonny Dundee;
So we'll store up a lauch when thochts aye come stealin'
O' the day that we spent Bazaarin' at Tealin'.

H Lamont, 4 September 1909

Tealing Dovecot, built 1595

CHAPTER 6
20TH CENTURY COMMUNITY LIFE,
MAJOR EVENTS & FOND MEMORIES

This century, perhaps more than any other has seen enormous changes take place. We can easily forget that it is only relatively recently that electricity, telephones, cars, television, public transport, supermarkets, cinemas and home ownership etc. became freely accessible to ordinary folk. In the space of 100 years, everyday life has changed beyond all recognition. And, over time, the old estates have released their grip on villages like Tealing and a much more independent way of living has emerged. Tealing folk who were born in the early 1900s have lived through all of this and two World Wars. They have watched the village and the land modernise, welcoming some of the changes and lamenting others. This chapter, largely through the eyes of those who lived it, captures just a snapshot of community life in Tealing, and the major events that affected the village, during the 20th century.

WORLD WAR LOSSES

The village paid a heavy toll during the First World War. The war memorial records that eleven young men fell -Private Joseph Barrie, Private James Bruce, Private John Cameron,

Lieutenant Archibald W R Don, Lieutenant Robert McPherson Don, Gunner Robert Marr, Private James B Morrison, Private William Philip, Private Alex R U rquhart, Private David Urquhart and Lance Corporal David N Winter. In 1921 the war memorial was dedicated at a well-attended and very moving ceremony which is more fully reported in Chapter 2.

Tealing War Memorial.

Mr Robert Don of Tealing House lost two sons in the Great War, Archibald at Salonika in 1916 and Robert, elsewhere in Greece, in 1917. He commissioned a memorial seat to the memory of his two sons, which still remains in Tealing, placed just outside the Old Post Office. In 1915, just one year before he died, the young soldier Archibald Don poignantly wrote: "How shall we mourn these dead, so rich in dying; long shall I weep who living were so fair? Singing they went through life, shall we go sighing? Smiling in death, can we not also dare? The memorial also lists four local men who died during World War 11 -Flight Sergeant R Jack, Naval Sergeant H Jack, A B J Johnston and Corporal L Mackie

TEALING HOUSE

Tealing house was owned successively by the Maxwells of Tealing from the 15th century, the Scrymseours from 1704 and the Fothringham Scrymseours from 1826. It would appear that when Robert Don (of the Don Buist Brothers family) took possession of Tealing House in 1913, the property, for the first time in hundreds of years, ceased to be part of the associated estate. At that time, the Estate of Tealing remained in the ownership of the Fothringhams. Robert Don and his wife had five sons. As reported above, the two youngest, who both served in the Black Watch, were killed in World War 1.Their brother, Alan Campbell Don, was ordained in the Anglican Church. He was Provost of the St Paul's Cathedral in Dundee from 1921 to 1931 and later became Dean of Westminster, after a spell as Chaplain to the Archbishop of Canterbury. He was made a Knight Commander of the Royal Victorian Order and played a considerable part in the Coronation of Queen Elizabeth 11.

Records indicate that Edmund C Cox occupied the house from about 1923, although the date that he took ownership is unclear. The valuation roll for 1935/36 attributes ownership to the Trustees of the late Edmund C Cox and shows the occupier as Mrs Eliza Dowall Cox. The Cox family history states that Mr Cox died in 1931 in Tealing House. His wife continued to live there until her death early in the war. Mrs Cox' grandson, Mr Ivor Guild, remembers visiting the house regularly as a child. He recalls that, although Mrs Cox lived alone, she had a considerable staff that included a retired gamekeeper/chaffeur, head gardener, under gardener, three garden boys, a cook, kitchen maid, table maid, three house maids and a ladies maid. Mr Guild's sister and other children from Dundee were evacuated to Tealing House when war broke out, but returned after about six months when it appeared that Dundee was not going to be bombed. In 1940 Tealing House was used as billets for the WAFFs until their accommodation was ready for occupation at Sheilhill and, for a period, it was also used as an officer's mess for Tealing Airfield.

In 1944, Mr William Bowie purchased the property. He ran a market garden in the grounds for many years. At its peak, 24 men were employed. The Evening Telegraph reported in 1949 that" cauliflowers take top place. Other crops include lettuces, peas, beans and tomatoes. Produce goes to Dundee, Aberdeen, Glasgow and wherever there is a ready market". Mr Bowie employed four men at that time, but found the scarcity of casual labour a problem. Another obstacle was the lack of youth on the land. "They all seem to want collar and tie jobs nowadays" Mr Bowie told the reporter.

By the time ownership transferred to Mr G. Thomson in 1988, Tealing House had become quite derelict and the market garden had long since ceased trading. The house and other associated buildings were accorded Listed Building status (Category B) in 1989, and since then, Mr Thomson has fully restored the property.

AGRICULTURE AND FARMING

The last Statistical Account highlighted the many changes that have taken in place in farming over the last one hundred years. It said "the land and farms of Angus directly employ about one tenth of the working population and, indirectly, affect the prosperity of many more. The trend during the 20th century has been for fewer and fewer workers to be employed on the land because of the gradual introduction of mechanisation and because of depressed economic conditions, particularly between 1918 and 1939.

Angus for the last two hundred years has been very much an arable county, producing cereals, root crops and grass which were largely converted into fat cattle and sheep. Between 1939 and 1965 there was a reduction of nearly 20,000 acres of pasture in Angus because of the ability of modern implements to reclaim land that had previously proved too difficult". The writer, Mr Norman Turner, also reported that the previous forty years (1928-1968) had seen an increase in "farming for the factory". He said that the factories at Montrose, Forfar, Carnoustie and Dundee for the processing of raspberries, strawberries, peas, broad beans, carrots and brussel sprouts had encouraged the popularity of those crops, most of which were grown under contract.

Writing more specifically about Tealing, also in 1968, the Rev James Kidd said, " the extensive use of machinery has completely changed farming. The combine harvester can be made to work around the clock and driers complete the process. The larger farms own machines and those without simply bring in the contractor who quickly disposes of grain and bales the straw. Bothies which housed four or five single men 30 years ago, now stand empty or house one family.

Farms are owned privately and twelve range from 200 to 700 acres. Mixed farming, mostly barley, seed potatoes and soft fruit obtains on the holding; there is only one dairy herd of 60 milch cows and no breeding herds but beef cattle are grazed on the larger farms, with seasonal sheep on the rough hill grass and wintering on the lower ground. One part of the airstrip provides facilities for a piggery with a stock of 3000. Also making use of this land lost to tillage is a broiler chicken establishment rearing a quarter of a million birds. A haulage contractor with a small fleet transports livestock".

Balkemback (one of the larger farms with 750 acres) has been in the Duncan family since 1881. The previous tenant was Mr George Langlands who had 23 children, many of whom are buried in Tealing Churchyard. Ian Duncan recalls "my grandfather Walter Gagie Duncan came to Balkemback in 1881 at the age of 19. At that time he was a tenant of the Douglas & Angus Estate owned by Earl Home of Coldstream in the Borders. He had 12/14 men in regular employment, supplemented by Irish workers during the harvest and at other busy times. The farmhouse also had two maids for domestic duties, There were 12 horses for heavy work and another two for the lighter work. One of the first tractors in the area was our old Fordson, which came to Balkemback in 1917 and was driven by my father. The present farmhouse was built during 1911-13 to replace the original house because it was full of dry rot.

Tealing Home Farm in the 50's.

During the war, two Hurricane aircraft crashed near the farm steading with no loss of life but, tragically, later in the war a Dakota came down on the hill between Balkemback and Prieston, killing all four crew. In 120 years of farming here, the main change has been the dramatic reduction in the number of people employed on the land, largely due to mechanisation. Electricity came to twelve of the Tealing farms in 1948, when a supply line from Wellbank was installed by the North of Scotland Hydro Electric Board. Another big change is that the children of farmers are less inclined these days to want to continue the farming tradition, whereas up until the 1950's and 1960's it was almost taken for granted that they would take over".

David Goodfellow was the tenant of Balnuith Farm from 1929 until 1944. Although the family business was baking (Goodfellow & Steven of Dundee) he had an inclination to farm, and after studying agriculture at college in Glasgow from 1922 until 1926, he finally secured his first farm at Balnuith. His son John Goodfellow remembers that the first few years were very hard and the farm did not have its first profit until 1933. David Goodfellow moved from Tealing to East Newton in Arbroath. He was President of the NFU in 1962/63 and was awarded the CBE in 1967 for services to the Agriculture Industry.

Bryce Millar, who farms at Prieston, was born at the farm in 1932. He recalls that when he started farming they grew oats, turnip, grass and potatoes. During the war they were also compelled to grow flax. They fattened cattle and bred sheep and worked with four Clydesdale horses until 1951. His first tractor was a standard Fordson. It had no starter, lights or hydraulics and its top speed was 6 mph. It was fuelled by petrol until hot, then paraffin. Harvest was by binder and then built into stacks to be threshed during the winter months. Horse ploughs, drillers and harrows were also used. Potatoes were lifted by spinner digger and carted in a box cart to outdoor pits. They were then dressed by hand riddle. Work then was mostly manual. When the mechanisation of harvesting came, two of the earliest combine harvesters in Tealing were Massey Harris 726's -in 1951 at Over Finlarg and Nether Finlarg.

Charlie Young has 420 acres at Shielhill and 360 at Huntingfaulds. He took over the farm at Shielhill in 1941 and has seen many changes in almost 60 years of farming in the area. He recalls" only one farm in the area has remained in the same family for the last 100 years -the Duncans at Balkemback, now owned by Ian Duncan. And, one of the biggest farms was Mr Bell's at Balnuith -before its size was reduced to accommodate the building of the aerodrome. The land in Tealing then was owned by two principal estates the Earl of Home (Douglas & Angus) and the Fothringham Estate and all of the large farms were tenanted. Things changed dramatically when the Tealing estate was sold in 1937 to the Department of Agriculture and over the years the majority of the farms have become owner occupied.

One dramatic change that took place during the First World War was the felling of 400 acres of woodland between Lumley Den and Huntingfaulds. Farm land has changed hands during prosperous periods and the depression in the 20s was very hard felt in Tealing. At the end of the Second World War Smedley had factories in Dundee and Coupar Angus and, for about 25 years, they encouraged local vegetable production. Initially the peas were carted to the factory on the Kingsway but Smedleys then provided a viner and they were processed as they were picked. Then, when mechanisation improved, six local farmers combined to buy 2 viners, but in 1972, Smedleys withdrew and the growing of peas largely stopped".

Tealing Hall

There have been two Tealing Halls during this century. The first one, a large timber hall, opened on 24 June 1913 with a concert and dance. It was situated on the corner across from the Old Post Office at Balgray and, between then and 1947, when it was burnt to the ground, it was always very heavily booked. All of the community groups already mentioned elsewhere in this book (WRI, Guild, Cubs, Brownies, Scouts, Guides etc) met at the old hall. The records show, however, that it was also booked by the Farm Servants Union, the Young Men's Guild, the Home Guard, the Youth Fellowship, Bowling -and for concerts, weddings and weekend camps for the Boys Brigade and Cubs from Dundee.

The present Tealing Hall situated in Inveraldie was once the gymnasium, cinema and chapel for the aerodrome. It opened as the new community hall on 9 Feb 1949 and has continued to be the focal point for most community activities ever since. Over the years it has hosted gatherings of all the long-term community groups, and also, a badminton club, a country dancing club and the Tealing Football Club. Although Angus Council owns the Hall, various Hall Committees, with the generous support of local people and very little other financial support have run it over the years. On 5 April 1999, in the Courier, Angus Council Housing Committee praised the Hall Committee's "outstanding effort of raising £40,000, over the previous seven years, to upgrade and improve the property".

THE WHITE HOUSE TODHILLS

This was an inn situated opposite the end of Whitehouse Farm Road. It consisted of Ale and Porterhouse and livery stables where the horses were rested or changed on the journey between Dundee and Forfar. It made an imposing landmark, since it was a large two-storey building and was always freshly white washed. It was also sometimes referred to as the "Half-way House". Jim MacFarlane recalls" my family lived in the house for nearly a year during 1939 until No 8 Holding, Todhills was completed. As a child I remember the traffic passing only a few feet from our window. At that time it was mainly buses and David Callendar of Forfar lorries, which were regularly carrying material to construct the runways at Tealing Aerodrome. The house and out buildings were demolished by Dundee Contracting Company in early 1940 and the material was used to make the entry roads to Holdings 1-7 on the Forfar Road".

THE AERODROME

In 1941, when the MOD decided to build the Aerodrome at Tealing, several farms in the area lost large acreage. Those hardest hit were Balnuith (240 acres reduced to 90), Inveraldie, Moatmill, Kirkton of Tealing and Myreton of Claverhouse. Some compensation was paid but it was not substantial. Mrs Ethel Hunter (nee Beattie) recalls " my parents, James and Jessie Beattie bought Inveraldie Farm in 1922. In July 1940 Air Ministry Officials called at the farm to tell my father that, as our farm was the first on level ground outside Dundee and in the interests of national security -they wanted to erect poles at regular intervals in our fields to prevent enemy gliders from landing! Almost immediately we were invaded, not by the enemy, but by workmen trampling down our ripening grain. They couldn't wait until after it was harvested.

Early in 1941, the Air Ministry approached my father again an informed him that they were requisitioning the most suitable parts off the farm to build an airbase for fighter aircraft. They promised complete restoration of the land at the end of hostilities, but this never happened".

No. 56 Officer Training Unit eventually opened in Tealing in March 1942, equipped with Hurricanes, Masters and some Lysanders. Pilots often had to contend with fog and bad visibility and, because of the Sidlaws at the West, night flying was impossible. The number of pilots training at the unit varied from about 40 in 1942, reaching a peak of 150 in 1943.

49

It was at the aerodrome that Tealing's most famous visitor arrived. On 20 May 1942, a strange four-engined aircraft appeared in the circuit at Tealing. It was one of the first Russian TB7s to visit Britain and it brought Vyacheslav Molotov, Russian Foreign Minister and Deputy Chairman of the State Committee of Defence, on a military mission to meet with Winston Churchill at Chequers. A local WAAF Sargeant remembers seeing the giant TB7 parked on the runway at Tealing. "Britain didn't have anything like it at the time and we were all stunned by the sheer size and presence of it" she said. "There was little pomp and circumstance, the priority was to ensure that Molotov's arrival and departure went smoothly". Tealing airfield was probably chosen to attract as little attention as possible to the visit. Molotov was given the choice of two aircraft in which to continue his journey to England. The one he did not select, as later revealed by Sir Archibald Hope, Senior Controller of Fighter Command in Scotland in 1942, crashed in flames in the Vale of York, killing various members of Molotov's staff and senior RAF personnel. Molotov arrived safely in London for the signing of the Anglo-Russian Treaty, 26 May 1942.

The Russian TB7 on the runway at Tealing.

In October 1943 the name of the Tealing unit was changed to 1 Tactical Exercise Unit (TEU) under Combat Training Wing, specialising in air firing and evasive action. By January 1944 the TEU was operating up to 110 aircraft. In February 1944, RAF Tealing exchanged 40 Hurricanes for 38 Spitfires from Grangemouth. Just prior to D-Day, 1 TEU at Tealing was put on operational readiness to re-enforce the regulars in the unlikely event of a counter attack from Norway, but the unit was stood down on June 15. The TEU disbanded on 31 July 1944, but during this final month it was host to a large number of Dakotas which were being used to enable locally based troops to practice embarkation. On one day alone, 90 Dakotas arrived from the Cotswolds. In August 1944, Tealing was taken over by Flying Training Command, 9(P) AFU. It disbanded on 21 June 1945 and was placed on care and maintenance under the wing of RAF Montrose.

THE TEALING BOMBS

It was springtime in the early 1940's that the first bombs were dropped in the Tealing area in the field between Leyshade and Myreton Farm (on Leyshade Farm ground). No one was injured and the target was never established. Tealing Aerodrome was not yet operational, although the line of .the three bombs would have been on target if it had been. Jim MacFarlane recalls "later that same year, another four bombs were dropped at Todhills the first on my father's land -Alex MacFarlane No 8 Holding and the other three on Mr Alex Scott's land, Newmains of Tealing. The target on this occasion was a searchlight close to Mr Scott's farm travelling east to west. The explanation given was that the plane had to release it's bomb load early to gain height and avoid hitting the Sidlaws. Again no one was hurt, but the first bombs reduced one of our hen houses to firewood and toppled a good few others. The plane was shot down in the Monifieth area and the pilot was taken to Ashludie Hospital for treatment. He was guarded by Mr H Smith, N07 Holding, Todhills". Jessie Mudie reports that six bombs were also dropped at Huntingfaulds in March 1941 -fortunately with no loss of life.

PRISONERS OF WAR

After the Second World War ended, captured German and Italian prisoners were billeted at a camp in the former WAFF quarters at Shielhill. In 1949, many of them returned to East and West Germany, some to be discharged from the Army, although many others decided to remain in Scotland. Joseph Hornung, who decided to stay, recalls" I was taken prisoner of war in March towards the end of the war by American Troops. When the Americans left we were transferred to British custody. Work consisted of agricultural camps in Cornwall and Devon, draining and industrial work at Newton Abbott. I spent 4/6 weeks at Errol prior to arriving at Shielhill, Tealing in February 1948. I worked mainly on farms, planting saplings, and doing any other work, wherever needed.

Conditions at the camp were basic but comfortable and everyone was treated well. At this time we more or less had civilian status. There were no restrictions and we enjoyed camp evening entertainment, visiting Dundee and having outside entertainers who provided programmes and dancing on many weekends. While at Tealing I had the chance to stay on or go back home to East Germany, but I decided to stay a year to earn a copper or two. However, that year, I met my future wife, a Dundee girl, at a Sunday night dance in the Empress Ballroom. When I saved some money, I bought clothes to send to my mother.

Peem (Jim) Reid, at Over Finlarg asked me to consider working for him on a permanent basis. I liked the atmosphere at Finlarg and decided to accept the offer. At first I shared a Bothy with 3 other countrymen. On marrying in 1951, we moved to our first cottage, but there was no electricity or luxuries then. I spent many happy years at Over Finlarg and both my daughters were members of the Tealing Guides and participated in community activities. I was presented with the Long Service Medal (proudly displayed) by the Earl of Strathmore at the Angus Show in 1979. I retired in April 1991 after 43 years at Over Finlarg and now live in Dundee, spending much of my time at my allotment. Preparing the soil, sowing and planting, then watching the results throughout the seasons remains very close to the heart".

Mr Egon Rode, who is now settled in Dundee, had a similar experience except that he returned to East Germany to be discharged from the Army before returning to settle in Scotland. Charlie and Margaret Young at Shielhill have fond memories of these times and recall that the prisoners of war were largely hard working, reliable and friendly. They have kept in touch with one man who did return to Germany and he has visited Scotland several times now with his family.

TEALING WOMEN'S GUILD (ESTABLISHED **1909**)

Mrs Christina Campbell recalls "I can remember very clearly the first night I went to the Guild. It was a very stormy night of strong winds and showers of hail and sleet. Mrs Miller, late of Moatmill, took me in her car along with Mabel and Mrs Carrie. We met in the vestry because we had a vacancy in the church and Reverend Harkness had just left (1957). The vestry was a small dismal room with poor lighting no heating and it was so cold that night. The guest that night was a missionary from Afghanistan and I was enthralled with her talk, life there was so hard for women. We took our own cups and Mrs Miller provided an electric kettle with water for our tea. The plug unfortunately was in the church!

At that time we were having talks with delegates from the Presbytery of Dundee, who were so determined that we join with Auchterhouse Church. Our last meeting with the Presbytery lasted four hours until we got permission to call a new minister for a period of 5 years. Before the Rev. Smith arrived, 8 members of the Guild cleaned and scrubbed the whole manse from the attic floor to the ground floor. When Mrs Smith arrived, the Guild was held in the manse, much more cheery and comfortable. I remember one particular night when our speaker failed to turn up, and I was asked to speak about my experiences working in the Balmoral Estate. This was a bit of an ordeal for me, but the end product was quite a success.

When houses were built in Inveraldie and a hall opened there, in the early fifties, the Guild moved to Tealing Hall. Members remained static for sometime, but in spite of much publicity, we failed to attract young members. We had an outing in the summer and sales of work or concerts in the wintertime, to contribute funds for church. When the Rev. J Kidd arrived we bought a more suitable and modern bungalow in Huntingfaulds Road because the old manse was so big, old fashioned and difficult to maintain. When we joined with Murroes Church, I was happy with the arrangement as Murroes Church was a beautiful church, but we had a problem -would we join Murroes Guild or try to persuade Presbytery to allow us to carry on at Tealing? I wrote to all the governing bodies asking for permission, which was freely granted, so we continued as Tealing Guild. Unfortunately the members are much less now. But, during the many years I attended, found the Guild very friendly and I enjoyed most of the programmes and working as a delegate on social responsibly, Home missions and Foreign missions and attending General Assembly. Although I am unable to attend Guild meetings now I am still am Honorary President and proud to be so".

TEALING **WRI** (ESTABLISHED **1924**)

At its height Tealing WRI was the most successful community group in Tealing, if levels of membership determine success -which peaked at around 120. Women of all ages attended regularly to enjoy a very varied programme of events, demonstrations and good company. Over the years, the branch competed in many categories at Forfar, bringing home the Cup on a few occasions and winning many individual categories. In 1949 the Evening Telegraph reported" on the southern fringes of the 'drome stands the home of Mrs D M Miller, who takes a keen interest in the WRI movement. Her enthusiasm is especially marked for handicraft and designing work. Tealing WRI has won the Federation Cup for baking and handicrafts this year. The WRI's wedding gift to Princess Elizabeth are tapestries, drapings and such bedroom accessories as quilts, footstools and rugs. Branches throughout Scotland are combining their most skilled needlewomen to do the work".

A lengthy poem was penned to celebrate the WRI's 50th anniversary, a few verses follow: -

It's 50 years since the rural started
A longish time to go unthwarted
When women from all walk of life
Resolve to be a better wife

It was in the year of twenty-four
That Tealing first began to soar
A band of women cleverly knew
Of interesting work which they could do

I've heard them speak of rollicking fun
With the Tealing Toppers and plays they have done
I've heard of awkward moments too
When members landed in stew

To the ladies of the committee, I've the greatest respect
The spare time given freely, no pay to collect
A word of encouragement never goes amiss
Will gladden their hearts and fill them with bliss!

53

THE TEALING GUIDES (ESTABLISHED 1927)

The 1st Tealing Girl Guide Company started in 1927 with Miss Molly Mount of Balluderon as Captain. She became District Commissioner in 1944 prior to Mrs Margaret Young of Shielhill, 1945-1948.

Janet Murray recalls "I joined in 1937, the meetings were held on a Friday evening and the Captain was Miss Maggie Paterson, who took over from Molly Mount. In the winter we were kept busy doing badge work, learning knots, first aid, morse code, flag signalling, sewing, knitting and country dancing. As we had no electricity then, just paraffin lamps, we had to be very careful if we had ball games. So they were left for the long clear evenings when we could play outside. During the summer evenings we would collect wild flowers and tree leaves, learn their names, collect firewood, cut turf and make camp fires where we would cook sausages on sticks. The highlight of the year was Guide Camp when we had a week away to put our skills to the test. When war broke out we would meet on a Saturday morning to collect Sphagnum Moss at Petterden, which was passed on to the Red Cross for use in dressings".

The Summary of Work records 1936-44 show that the group was very active. Their activities also included attending a rally in the Caird Hall Dundee when Lady Baden Powell visited in 1936, Coronation Rallies in 1937, concerts and fund raising for the Auchterhouse Sanatorium and knitting blanket squares for the Red Cross.

The Company was suspended in 1948 and then re-started in 1961, with 18 girls, at Tealing Hall. The Lieutenants were Eva Robertson and Zena Wylie. During the sixties, membership at the Murroes dropped and the company became the 1st Murroes/Tealing Girl Guide Company in 1970, continuing to meet in Tealing. Eva (now Acting Guide Guider) remembers "the programme was similar to the early years with the exception of war service. Today the girls are much more aware of global issues and help with aid to various charities and war/natural disaster areas. Things have changed over the years. The girls have other interests and, unfortunately, the numbers have dropped to just eight".

Today's guides wish that more girls would get involved because "it is really fun, interesting and exciting" and they "hope for peace for Guides in troubled countries". The current leaders are Lynn Hally and Linda Reid and the District Commissioner is Sheila Crichton of Wellbank.

HALLY'S GARAGE

Mr John Hally was born in 1928 and first came to Tealing in 1935. He recalls "the winters in the 30's and 40's were much more severe and we were often cut off for days

Hally's Garage, Winter 1947.

with many vehicles trapped in the snow. We would have people needing shelter and, on one occasion, we had about 30 stranded travellers in the Smithy keeping themselves warm and eating eggs pickled for the winter. We started selling petrol in 1935 from' a hand operated pump which could supply 6 different brands. The price was around one shilling and seven pence per gallon. My father and brother being Farriers as well as Blacksmiths, shod the big work horses from the farms as well as repairing farm implements. All welding was done in the Forge. Gas and electric welding followed in later years. Early radios were called wireless sets and were operated by battery as very few houses had electricity. Locals would bring their accumulators along to the garage to be recharged. We stopped selling petrol in April 1990".

THE CREATION OF THE SMALLHOLDINGS 1937

In 1937, the estate of Tealing was sold to the Department of Agriculture, for £23,497, to meet the death duties of Thomas Stuart Fothringham. The Department of Agriculture then leased the land in Tealing for 41 smallholdings, ranging in size from 5 to 50 acres. About six farms were broken up in this way.

Writing about the smallholdings in Tealing in 1949, the evening Telegraph reported "in the Todhills direction to the north of the parish, stands the holding of Mr & Mrs J Campbell which they have quaintly named "Tinkletap". Their main line is chicken farming. Mrs Camp bell bears the brunt of this work, while her husband grows the corn to feed the hens and tends their nine acres of potato land. They also have a few cows, calves, horses and a pig. Their stock of hens runs to 2000. In this year's hatching season they produced about 14,000 chicks. Mr & Mrs Campbell have been on their Todhills holding for about 14 years. One of their near neighbours is Mr Alec Keir who goes in for dairy farming. His land runs to 50 acres and he has 16 milk cows and grows corn, potatoes and turnips".

In 1968 the Statistical Account said, " There are three main groups of smallholdings in Angus, the largest group being in Mains, Strathmartine and Tealing. They are the property of the Department of Agriculture, Fisheries and Food and are let to tenants. They are worked full-time, part-time or spare-time. Many of the larger holdings are well equipped viable units. Recently there has been a tendency to amalgamate some of the smaller ones as the opportunity arises. Some of the smaller units near Dundee specialise in the production of fruit, flowers and vegetable, selling at the farm gate".

The Clark Family at No.18 Holding recalls" the soft fruit industry played a major part
in the life of the Tealing smallholder. Most 5/10-acre holdings had both strawberries and
raspberries. In the early days most strawberries went to the canneries, then the freezers
started up and you could select the best berries in punnets for the supermarkets. The
weather often decided whether the farmer made a good profit or not, Two or three rainy
days could destroy a lot of fruit. The berry season gave local school children and adults
the chance to make some extra cash as pickers were always needed, but now machinery
has taken over. Many happy days were had in the berryfields".

THE 57TH ANGUS SCOUT GROUP (ESTABLISHED1937)

There have been scouts in the Tealing area since 1937. Until 1970 they met at the scout hut
at Myreton, but by the late sixties the youth population was concentrated in Tealing and
Wellbank. This coincided with the Murroes Scout Hut being sold to a transport contractor.
In 1971 the 57th moved their meeting place to Tealing Hall and retained their maroon
neckers. The Hall was not ideal for such an energetic group of boys, so the derelict tennis
pavilion was bought from the council for a token sum and was refurbished to become the
Tealing Scout Hut. It opened in 1972.

Over the years the weekly troop meeting has lasted for 2 hours and has included games,
training and projects. Graham Campbell remembers" some of the games were of a very
physical nature; hucky ducky, British bulldogs and chalk rugby were very effective in
exhausting them -a pre-requisite to embarking on Scout training skills, such as map and
compass work, knots, lashings and first aid. The annual camp was the highlight of the year
and the activities did not change much over the years. They would include the construction
of a monkey bridge over the river, skinning rabbits, backwoods cooking, sleeping out,
canoeing and swimming in "dookers and auld sannies" and the chant of Ogi, Ogi, Ogi
around the camp fire. The scouts would sit around the open fire eagerly listening to yarns
and far-fetched tales of fictitious characters. Memorable experiences for the boys of the
57th". The 57th won many prizes, bringing home the Angus County Area Flag in 1953,1961
and 1976, the Angus Camping Trophy in 1984 and competing in the Scottish Scouting
Competition in the same year. Scout numbers used to average around 25, but they have
declined over the years to single figures. The Scouts still meet at the Murroes School but the
Beavers and Cubs have closed through lack of numbers."

James R Burns & Sons, Haulage Contractors, Tealing (Established 1940's)

This family firm was established by James R Burns Snr in the 1940's and is carried on today
by James R Burns Jnr under the name of Burns Transport. Dave Burns recalls "the business
began with one vehicle, increasing eventually to five articulated vehicles. Initially,
transportation of livestock dominated the workload ie. hauling store and fat cattle to the

Marts. As the pig industry grew Muir of Pert, Tealing and Crail, Fife became well known in this field. From these centres 400 weaned pigs were transported weekly to Aberdeen, Dyce and Edinburgh Marts. Pigs were also collected from FMC Contracts for delivery to Ayr, Sheffield and Carlisle. One aspect of farming now gone from these parts was the cultivation of sugar beets. The beet was hauled from farm to the factory at Cupar and this covered a three-month period.

Eventually farming diversified with regard to transportation. Farmers bought their own floats and transported the animals to the Marts. Livestock transportation had disadvantages as vehicles could be sitting at the Marts for several hours waiting for "bought cattle returns" to take back to the farms. This tied the driver at the Marts, unable to do other jobs and it was not economic. It was time to move on to bulk grain and potato haulage and canned food -general transportation as it is today".

THE LOCAL REGISTRAR 1944-1984

For generations, registration of births, deaths and marriages was done locally by the school headmaster or minister. But this was not always the case. In 1944, the Registrar's Office could be found at 37 Holdings at the home of Mrs Jane Clark, who filled the role. Her daughter-in-law, Mrs Wilma Clark, took over the responsibility when Mrs Clark senior retired. She recalls "in the early days, up to World War 11,births were mostly at home and marriages were either at home, in the local church or in the village hall. All of these events had to be registered in the parish. Deaths could be registered either at the parish of death or the parish of residence. However, things changed in the 1960's as small parishes were amalgamated, thus reducing the number of registrars required and, in 1984, all rural offices were closed and business transferred to Dundee office. The job was eventful and varied, the local registrar having no set hours for business and having to accommodate the public at any time".

CORONATION CELEBRATIONS 1953
One of the most remarkable mementoes of Tealing is the cine film of the village gala day to celebrate the Coronation of Queen Elizabeth on 2 June 1953. The film was commissioned by the WRI and, over about fifteen minutes, it shows marvellous snapshots of the fun had on the day. Miss E. Bowie recalls that it was a very cold day, but in spite of that, parents and children took part in an outdoor programme that included a fancy dress competition for the children and a sports competition for adults and the children. The fancy dress parade featured all things patriotic -many kings and queens, with one wee boy even encasing the back of his tricycle in a Union Jack! Councillor Mudie, the Rev Harkness and Mrs Millar from Moatmill can all be seen busying themselves with the proceedings. Miss Bowie issues ice creams to eager children and they were all given commemorative coronation mugs. A celebratory lunch was had in Tealing Hall and the many helpers and participants are depicted, clearly having a good time. A television was also set up in the hall so that the

proceedings in Westminster could be viewed. The cine film has been converted on to video and will be retained in the village archive.

TEALING TENNIS CLUB 1950-1958

Tealing Tennis Club was formed in 1950 at a meeting held at the tennis courts, which the RAF had vacated after the war ended. A Committee was appointed and Mrs Miller, a very enthusiastic lady, was elected the first President. The first hardy souls to enlist included Mrs Miller of Moatmill, Councillor Mr George Mudie and Jessie Mudie and the Rev. Charles B Harkness. The pavilion needed some renovation and a team of volunteers soon had the building spic and span. After the first two years, the Club played friendly matches against near neighbours Longforgan and Invergowrie. They then joined the Midlands Tennis League, Fifth Division. Ron Campbell recalls" although we did not win many matches, we really enjoyed the experience of playing at courts such as Morgan, Craigielea, Dundee High School, Longforgan, Invergowrie and the YMCA courts". Unfortunately, support dwindled and the Club disbanded in the late fifties.

TEALING DRAMATIC CLUB 1950-1960

The club started around the beginning of 1950 and lasted most of that decade. It was the idea of the late Mr & Mrs George Mudie of Newbigging and the late Mrs Miller of Moatmill. It drew a large membership of men and woman of all age, meeting every Monday evening. Mrs Beatrice Mitchell recalls "happy times were had by all. But there were headaches too, when "lines" had to be learned. Usually it was Scots comedy one-act plays we performed, doing three at a time for our annual concert, which was often in aid of W.R.!. funds. Other districts asked us to come along with our show. This we greatly enjoyed, as performing to the home audience was more nerve racking! After a while we became more adventurous in staging three and four act plays, perhaps the best one was "Beneath the Wee Red Lums".

We also joined the Scottish Community Drama Association and I recall that four of us went to Edzell for a drama school weekend thinking we knew it all, but were soon put right about acting! A lot of hard work went into the Dramatic Club from others in the community, making props and backstage work. Real community spirit of old. I spent a lot of happy times at the club, where I met, acted with and fell in love with my late husband Rab. The good old days without a doubt!"

TEALING YOUTH CLUB 1950-1963

The club was formed in the early fifties and it had junior, intermediate and senior sections. For recreation, various games, drama, competitions, quizzes, dancing and outings took place. Halloween and Christmas were always celebrated with parties and the Youth Club was the first in the village to hold a Christmas party for the senior citizens. The annual bus drives for parents and senior members were always a good day out. N an Wilkie recalls "

58

senior members and leaders attended summer educational camps at various locations, including the lovely Dalguise House on the banks of the Tay in Perthshire". Other youth clubs met in Tealing Hall in later years. The leader in 1984 was Jennifer Ramsay who lived at North Powrie. At that point, the club was run under the supervision of Dundee District Council.

TEALING TENANT'S ASSOCIATION 1957-1972

In 1946, several young local couples approached Councillor George Mudie seeking help to obtain rented accommodation in the area. As a result, Angus County Council agreed to convert 10 huts at the aerodrome, previously used by the RAF, into 20 temporary houses. They were ready for occupation in 1948 and were to be followed by new and permanent housing, ready for occupation in 1953/54, and to be known as Inveraldie. Willie Wilkie writes" substantial rent increases were implemented at the new development, so we formed the Tealing Tenant's Association to argue for modification, with a view to forming associations, not just in Tealing, but elsewhere in Angus. The inaugural meeting was held on 17 March 1957, office bearers appointed were Willie Wilkie, Vic Rankin and Dunc Murray, with a committee of twelve".

Those involved were further annoyed at the cheek of the Council sending the rent collector in a Rolls Royce taxi not very sensitive! Willie continues" after a great deal of spadework, committees were formed in several areas, with representation on the Angus Tenant's Association. On 29 April 1957, more than 400 banner carrying demonstrators marched on Forfar. The tactic proved successful and the outcome was a modified increase in rent and rates throughout Angus. Tealing Tenants Association continued to function for a number of years, finally being wound up

The Rent Collector's Rolls Royce

a special meeting of the Committee in September 1972". Willie's wife Jessie went on to become an active Community Councillor and, in 1999, was the first Community Councillor in Angus to be presented with a certificate by the Provost, in recognition of 25 years of service to the local community.

NEW HOUSES AT INVERALDIE 1954

One of Tealing's most elderly residents, Miss Mabel McLean aged 88 years, recalls " the family moved to Inveraldie Farm in 1937 when Beattie was the farmer, moving to Nether Finlarg in 1939. From Nether Finlarg we moved to Bowie's where Dad did odd jobs. On retiring, the family moved back to Inveraldie Farm. Because of Dad's death in 1949, we moved to the Huts (at the aerodrome). In 1954, we got a low door, no stairs, home in

Inveraldie. Mother marvelled at the wonder of electricity and moved from room to room exclaiming that she would no longer have the dirty, smelly, tilly lamp globes to clean! I still have the same fireplace and electric cooker and only recently gave away my girdle".

TEALING POLICE STATION 1960-1969

PC David Oram was the last "village bobby" to live at the Tealing Station, just off the Forfar Road across from Tealing Wood, from 1960 until 1970. As a young man, he was posted to Tealing at very short notice and arrived in October 1960 with his wife Dorothy and their two daughters, aged 2 and 5. Being in sole charge of the station was a 24 hours per day responsibility, with one day off weekly and long hours on call. He was lucky enough to be provided with a black Police BSA 200cc motor scooter which really helped him get around his large and busy beat but he recalls that, most of the time, he was frozen to the seat!

His responsibilities were varied. Attending road accidents, sudden deaths, shotgun, firearms and explosives licences, handling and investigating offences, stray dogs, patrolling the area, animal matters, bike safety at the school etc. Fortunately, he found the people of Tealing to be "law abiding and well behaved" -most of the problems involved visitors or those just passing through. PC Oram particularly remembers dealing with many accidents on the road between Lumley Den and the Shiellhill Road, which, even back then, was dubbed an accident black spot. On at least two occasions vehicles landed spectacularly close to the police station and he literally "put his head outside the door". of the station to deal with them.

A fair bit of time was spent in contact with the local farmers. " I got to know practically every farmer on my beat and found them quiet, hard working members of the district, not that easy to get to know, as they were not what one would term the" gushie type". In the mid -sixties PC Oram had to deal with one of the biggest outbreaks of swine fever in Scotland at the piggery and had to hurriedly learn about the role of the police in such situations. Dogs worrying sheep was also a recurring problem and chasing animals through fields certainly kept him fit and healthy.

Policing was what one might term" creative" in those days. He recalls having to deal with 6 young men who had been thrown off the bus in Tealing for being rowdy. They were stranded and desperate for a lift into Dundee. Much to their relief, PC Oram and a colleague, PC Goldie, offered them a lift in the police van. Only they didn't mention that Dannie the police dog was already occupying the van, until they had locked them in. Apparently, Dannie growled at them all the way back to Dundee and there was not a further cheep from any of the young rowdies. Very effective and no paper work to do!

'Towards the end of his period in Tealing, policing methods changed and the one-man stations were gradually withdrawn. PC Oram's wife Dorothy penned a poem about the demise of the village bobby, just a few verses follow:

> Year in he tends his beat with pride,
> And tries to take things in his stride,

He's just an honest working lad,
Dealing with the good and bad.

He copes with property, lost and found,
Cow with staggers, dogs to the pound.
Children lost, sheep on the road,
Permits for guns, out of gauge-load,

Many a sad day he must get through,
Dealing with accidents, injuries too,
People left with an aching heart,
He must show compassion, yet stand apart.

But the cry today is amalgamation,
One man, one job, in re-organization.
The man's category we must select,
The computer says -reject -reject,
So the country bobby he must go,
It's for efficiency you know!

OTHER FOND MEMORIES

LOCAL SHOPPING

Before the big supermarkets in Dundee and Forfar opened Tealing had it's own fair share of small local shops. Mrs Wilkie's house and shop (now demolished) was built in 1924 and for the next decade was the first house on the Dundee/Forfar Road after the Mains Toll House. Mrs McFarlane at No. 8 Holding ran a sweetie and lemonade shop and the Smiths at Woodside also had a small shop. At one point, long ago, there was even a chip shop in Tealing, ran by Mr Mudie on the Newbigging Road. There was for a while two post offices - at Inveraldie, where the pub now is, and at the Tealing Post Office and General Store run by Mr & Mrs Todd at Balgray, across from the old Tealing Hall.

There had been a post office at the second site for 100 years. The entry in the Forfarshire Directory of *1887/88* said "Post Office, Balgray, Tealing -William Marr Postmaster. Letters arrive at 9.00am and are despatched at 2.30pm. The nearest money-order office is in Dundee".

The Old Tealing Post Office and Teashop.

Jack and Florrie Todd ran the post office for 21 years until it closed in February 1976. The Evening Telegraph reported at the time "it has the typical rural versatility, somehow finding space for ginger beer and boiled ham, spanners, hammers and electric lamps, cakes and biscuits. At one time Mrs Todd ran her own teashop, with freshly-laundered tablecloths, butter and jam in round glass dishes, table knives and home made scones and shortie, often freshly hot from the oven. And delight of delights -real flowers in vases.

En route from Glamis, the little princesses Elizabeth and Margaret are reputed to have called at the village shoppie for the purchase of chocolate and sweets. For special parties Toddy's teashop could put on morning coffee, lunch and high tea. But business was too erratic, dead in winter and so busy in summer with berry-pickers and weekend tourists that the Todd family ran the risk of exhaustion. Its sad news for city ramblers and walkers across the Sidlaw Hills that the persistent door-bell on the store will sound its last knell".

When the post office in the room behind the Inveraldie Inn closed, Colin Paton opened a sub-post office in his yard. It continued for a further seven years until it became part of the petrol station on the A 90. That petrol station, and the post office within it, closed just two years later. When the current Club petrol station opened they wanted to run the sub-post office again, but this was ruled against on the basis that the users would have to cross the A 90 on foot and this should not be encouraged.

"THE TEALING APPARITIONS"

Mrs Christina Camp bell tells the story "for a period in 1950, white apparitions, covered completely in white sheets, floated in and out of the trees whenever anyone came off the bus at Tealing Woods. Following up complaints, PC Middleton became involved and, in spite of his watchful eye over a period 3/4 weeks, didn't manage to solve the mystery. It eventually turned out that the "the ghosts" were mischievous local lads, the Morgan, Ramsay and Carrie boys, just fooling around!"

THE WINTER OF 1947

Miss Mabel McLean recalls "during the '47 winter when I was working in Dundee, one afternoon I met Mrs Fulton of Nether Finlarg who suggested that, due to the worsening weather, I should get the bus home soon. But by the time I left there were no buses, so I set off walking in my raincoat and wellies. I must have looked like a tattie-bogle! Once I got to Chalmers the tracks were covered over and, with the freezing fog, I lost my way, circling the field many times. Mind you, the currant loaf and one pound of steak in my bag was probably frozen too! Eventually, seeing footsteps over the dyke, I followed them and found my mother at the back door and my father at the front door of the house. It was a quarter to two in the morning!"

THE 1968 STATISTICAL ACCOUNT

Writing in 1968, the Rev. James Kidd reported that the population of Tealing had steadily declined between 1831 and 1931, but had started to pick up when the holdings were rented in the late thirties:

1901	615
1921	577
1931	515
1961	808

The average numbers of births, deaths and marriages had continued to decline and in 1968 was 15, 5 and 8. On housing, he reported that" farm cottages have been extensively brought up to modern standards as workers will no longer tolerate poor living conditions. Holdings have a house of four rooms, kitchenette and steading, brick built, now thirty years standing and sufficient for families of 2/3 children, which is the prevailing distribution. Council houses are from 2 rooms to five rooms. The smallest are equipped to suit the aged, many of whom live alone, while the larger are occupied almost entirely by city workers".

Regarding social amenities, the Rev Kidd said that, in 1968, there was relatively active local involvement in the Brownies, Cubs, Scouts, Guides, Senior and Junior Youth Clubs, Sunday School, the Men's Social Club, the Woman's Guild, the WRI and the Tenant's Association. But he added " since the introduction of television and the installation of electric power in every quarter, social activities have declined. The football team from ten years ago no longer functions and, as there is no commercial amusement, those who seek it may use a regular bus service to Dundee or Forfar, or travel by private cars, which a large majority owns. Community sense is divided between those who come from and work in the city and those who work the land. It is difficult to predict how the two streams of living will develop, by flowing into one, or striving to retain their separate identities".

CHAPTER 7
TEALING TODAY & OUR HOPES FOR THE FUTURE

Tealing today is a village where people can get the best of both worlds, enjoying all the benefits of country living within just a short drive of town and city amenities. The population has levelled out at around 500 and there is just enough new building, and changes in home ownership, to ensure that we retain enough young families to keep the primary school at the heart of the community. Membership of the church has reduced quite dramatically over the last two hundred years, in line with the rest of Scotland. Tealing is still dominated by working farms and all of the smallholdings are now privately owned. The skyline over the Sidlaws still features the Civil Aviation Authority Radio Station at Craigowl and the Angus Television Transmitter.

Apart from the farms, there are still a few businesses in the area. Rembrand Timber Ltd. at Shielhill Wood employs about 50 people at the company headquarters in Tealing. The business has grown steadily since it started 20 years ago and now has depots at several locations around Scotland. Rembrand trades in. timber, sheet materials and joinery products. Grampian Country Foods Ltd now runs the chicken broiler establishment at the old aerodrome. It employs four people and has about 250,000 birds at anyone time. The Muir of Pert piggery has been taken over by Scotpigs Ltd. an Aberdeenshire based company. It now employs 18 people and keeps 10,000 pigs. The only remaining shop in Tealing is within the Club petrol station on the A90 and there is a bar and lounge at the Inveraldie Inn.

The majority of residents who work are now employed in the surrounding towns and cities and there is a significant retired population. Although the numbers participating in the various community groups has reduced, Tealing Hall is still used almost daily and several local groups are sustained almost entirely by donations and fundraising. Events involving the children at Tealing Primary School are usually" standing room only". On leaving primary school the children move up to Forfar Academy, from where most of them go to jobs with training, further education or university.

We asked community representatives and group leaders to say something about the changes they have observed over the years and their hopes for the future of the village.

BESSIE COVENTRY, PRESIDENT TEALING WOMAN'S GUILD, HALLKEEPER, PRESIDENT OF THE WEDNESDAY CLUB AND TEALING COMMUNITY COUNCILLOR

Although it will be 50 years in December since I came to stay in Tealing from a neighbouring Parish, it is only during the past 15 years that I have taken a keen interest in what goes on in the community. When I came here we lived in the old RAF huts that were converted into houses until they built the present council houses, four years later, in 1954. At that time there were 2 mobile grocer vans and 2 bakers and 2 butchers used to come around 2-3 times a week. Plus there was a Bank of Scotland van once a week. There also used to be 3 small shops on the Forfar Road. Then a shop was built in Inveraldie -it had a License and a Post Office, until it was sold. The new owners turned it into the Inveraldie Inn with the shop made smaller at the back, until it changed hands a few times, then sadly we had no more local shops. Supermarkets going up in Dundee made it difficult for small shops to stay open. I think the biggest change was when the Forfar Road was made into a dual carriageway.

As President of the Guild and the Wednesday Club and being involved with the Tealing Hall and the Community Council, I would like to see more people in the community come along to some of the activities that go on. They don't know what they are missing out on.

MARGARET NAPIER, NAPIER SCHOOL OF DANCING

Born and brought up in the Tealing area, I have been involved with Highland Dancing since the age of three, starting off as a pupil in the nearby Murroes Hall. Over the years I have danced with Davie Glen and the Nickytammers in various locations throughout Scotland, and in the Palace Theatre in Dundee with Andy Stewart, Calum Kennedy, Johnny Victory and many others. I qualified as a dance teacher in 1968, starting off with a class in Tealing Hall, where I have been every Saturday afternoon ever since!

Very little has changed, except that I now have the daughters of former pupils (am I really that old?). For the last three years I have also been teaching line dancing in Tealing Hall. How enjoyable it is watching the children progress as the years go by, seeing some of them go on to qualify as teachers themselves and seeing the line dancers give it their all on Tuesdays and Wednesdays. What a great bunch they all are, including the parents of the children, past and present, and Ian Reid and Roy Beveridge who play for the displays. We get great support from so many local people. I hope we are still going strong for another thirty-two years!

MRS A RAMSAY, PRESIDENT, TEALING W.R.I

I moved to Tealing when I was married in 1961 and I was first introduced to the "Rural" in the 60's by my mother-in-law who was a founder member and first secretary of the

W.R.I. in 1924. Membership when I joined was around 100. Unfortunately through the years this has trickled down to under 30. Meetings are held once a month and in the early days the Rural was a meeting place where women of all ages could meet and enjoy an evening together. It's said that the W.R.I. now has the reputation of being an organisation for older women but try as we may we find it almost impossible to encourage young women to join us. The W.R.I. has much to offer with a wide variety of talks and

65

demonstrations, competitions, and many crafts to learn. Many Institutes have had to close because of low membership and unless we can increase our membership in the future, it seems inevitable that eventually Tealing W.R.I. will cease to exist. My hopes for the future of Tealing W.R.I. would be that more women will come along and help to support our organisation. We are now in our 75th year and I would like to think that the "Rural" will still be going strong for many years to come.

P.C. CHARLES REID ARCHIBALD (RECENTLY RETIRED)

It was around Christmas 1988 that I was appointed as the local Police Officer for the Tealing Area. Constable Ian McKenzie who had looked after the area for the past 8 years had previously filled this position. Prior to this time I had been in several areas of Dundee with various communities. In my time as the Local Policeman there has been little or no change to the area and the community. This has been a critical factor in my enjoyment of the area and community. The community is well established and sometimes change can effect even the youngest of community members. While the community does not change this allows the characters of the area to flourish in the village atmosphere.

My hope for the future of the area is that it continues to enjoy a fairly low crime rate and that the ever-growing house market does not single out Tealing and hence add to the population and the problems this brings. The community spirit has allowed me the joy of watching the young people of the area progressing through school and on to University / College or full time work and apprenticeships, some have even progressed to marriage and children of their own, starting the village cycle all over again.

The job I was involved in often placed me in positions of great sorrow and also elation for whatever reasons. The underlying spirit of the community helped these families and friends at this time of which I felt a great part. I would like to take this opportunity to for their support and assistance over the years, which aided in assisting my job extending friendships. I would like to wish the entire community a joyous and prosperous millennium as I venture on my own journey into retirement.

DR L E LUSCOMBE, RETIRED BISHOP OF BRECHIN AND TEALING SCHOOL BOARD MEMBER

It use to be said that to make a village into a community, four buildings were desirable, a church, a school, a shop and a pub but just two of them were essential. Kirkton of Tealing is an exception to that rule. I moved into the Kirkton from Dundee in 1988, and soon discovered a very real sense of community within the larger community of Tealing. No doubt this was why my late wife and I were able to settle easily into rural life. So much so, in fact, that we acquired a lair in the churchyard. Incidentally there has been a marked improvement in the standard of upkeep of the ground around the church in recent years. This may perhaps be because Angus District Council has more of a feel for this kind of thing in country districts than the city had. I have begun to find that it is a reciprocal feeling, for I now find myself increasingly drawn to Forfar for shopping easier (and free!) to park, and not much further away than Dundee. If only the junction with the dual carriageway were improved!

COUNCILLOR FRANK ELLIS, COUNCILLOR FOR SIDLAW WEST, ANGUS COUNCIL

I have represented the Parish of Tealing from 5th May 1994 when I was elected to represent Sidlaw Ward 31 on Tayside Regional Council. I still represent Sidlaw West, which includes Kirkton of Tealing up to Huntingfaulds. My observation over the years is that in partnership with the Community Council, School Board and Village Hall Committees, unlike the former days when we were within the Council Administrative Boundary of Dundee, the rural community has recognised that it has a voice of influence and is more determined to use it. The Tealing residents have taken ownership of Angus Council and it is my opinion that the residents feel valued by Angus Council.

My hopes for the future of Tealing is that together we can first, successfully in the near future resolve the vehicular and pedestrian safety issue of the A 90 / dual carriageway; secondly, ensure that the lovely environment we live in is protected for future generations and thirdly, encourage small businesses to invest in our area to ensure that rural Tealing is vibrant and there is employment opportunities for the residents who live there. My message to Tealing residents is that it has been a pleasure and honour to represent you from 1994 and I wish you all good health and prosperity in this New Millennium.

MARGARET TEALING HALL COMMITTEE

I came to Tealing when I got married forty years ago. Back then I think Tealing was a much smaller, friendly community. Everyone spoke to each other or if they were passing in a car, they waved. Everyone knew each other. Now Tealing has grown and changed and not necessarily for the better. There is not the same community spirit and the new residents don't seem to want to participate in village life. This is very noticeable when you look at how membership of the various groups has dropped. In the future I would like to see more community spirit and I hope that the younger ones will start to participate in the organisations to ensure that they carry on over the years. I hope that the village doesn't become just another commuter area and I also feel that more could be done for the children, as there seems little for them to do.

HELEN COUNCILLOR FOR SIDLAW EAST AND ANGUS COUNCIL

I share stewardship of the area with my fellow councillor, Frank Ellis, whose local connection stretches back a bit further than my own. Prior to being selected to stand in the Angus Council by-election on 25 November 1999, my knowledge of Tealing's history was

67

sketchy. I knew that in the recent past, as far as local government was concerned; it had been in Angus, then Dundee, and now Angus again, and that in the main, Tealing people preferred to be in Angus, retaining their own identity, rather than being swallowed up by the city. What I didn't appreciate was the rich history associated with the area in its own right and I am impressed with the way local residents work so hard in the community to safeguard your history.

With the economic constraints placed on councils nowadays, community projects will more than ever be community-led, but I believe that villages like Tealing, which already have a solid core of people rich in community spirit will rise to this challenge. My hopes for the future are that each community in my ward will retain its unique identity, while participating in the successful economy of Angus and I will work in partnership with other councillors, community councils, local organisations and residents to ensure that this happens.

KAY DENNIS, CHAIRPERSON, TEALING PRIMARY SCHOOL PARENT TEACHER ASSOCIATION

The PTA began in May 1990. I can well remember our very first fundraising event. It was a Jumble Sale held in October. It wasn't due to start until 7.00pm, but we arrived at 6.30pm to find the playground full of cars and people. It was quite frightening fighting our way through! When we got into the classroom where the sale was to be held there were faces peering in through the windows. We opened the doors and were almost trampled in the rush. It was worth it though as we raised £250.

We are a very successful fundraising committee. We subsidise buses for school outings, the trip to the pantomime at Christmas, to buy books, toys, prizes for sports day, Halloween etc. We also try to organise fundraising events that include the whole community. Our most recent was a Bingo night. We have two major fundraisers every year, a sponsored spell in the spring and a bingo night in the autumn. We also have a raffle at our AGM and cake and candy at sports day. My hope for the millennium is to continue to involve the parents and the local community in projects at the school.

IAN REID, FARMER AT NEWBIGGING AND CHAIRMAN OF THE HALL COMMITTEE

I came to Tealing in 1940, only one year old. One of my earliest memories is of being bathed in the sink (no luxury bathrooms in those days) and the water being either too hot out of the kettle or too cold. Ugh! At five I went to Murroes Academy where I made many friends and got a good education that prepared me for the world at large. I am sure that the Dominie missed his vocation though, for the way he wielded the stick would have been better used on cattle than on our backs!

Being of farming stock there was never any doubt about what I would do. I had started my apprenticeship at ten, feeding the cattle and having a shot on the old Fordson tractor, later to be replaced by the old Fergie. In 1903, my grandfather John Robertson of Blairgowrie, was one of the first four raspberry growers in Blair and so it was that we began to grow raspberries at Newbigging in 1946. As the crop became more and more important, we had to use outside pickers. In the 70's and 80's it seemed that half of Tealing helped pick the berries. Whole families came along -Mums and bairns during the day, joined by Dads at nights and weekends. I remember in particular the Chapman, Winter, Begg, Wilkie, Reoch, Paton, Morrison, Black, Watson, Motion and McIntosh families all being a great help, but there were many others. Without them, the crop would not have been gathered, so many thanks to all the "Tealing Berry Pickers".

Another early and vivid memory was the visit of the threshing mill. It was a big occasion on any farm and I will always remember the sight of the steam engine with the sparks flying out of the lum. Here again neighbours rallied to help out with "the Mull" and relatives from Alyth, Meigle and Kirrie also came along, making this a memorable occasion. Threshing mills have disappeared to be replaced by combines, balers and a host of other machines to do the work. Long ago there were no fancy weed killers or sprays, just all the good folks working hard together. These days we are left with a skeleton staff on the farms and a load of machinery. The two-way trade in produce and services with Dundee has totally disappeared.

On a recent visit to Tealing, one of the aircrew who had served at the Drome remarked that he hardly recognised the village at all after 55 years. He recalled that during wartime we had nothing but we had everything, meaning that there was a great community spirit then. I hope that the new millennium will rekindle that spirit in Tealing.

TEALING TODAY

Those then are the very mixed views and hopes of our community leaders. What do the younger generation think? Well, they are generally more hopeful and ambitious cynicism hasn't set in yet! In a competition run with Tealing Primary School pupils in 1998, the children were asked how they would like to see Tealing develop in the millennium. Perhaps predictably, they produced a long wish list of facilities they would like that included a leisure centre, a swimming pool, a theme park, a youth club and a gymnasium. One young lad had a vision of a brand new premier league football stadium outside Tealing School where all the famous teams would come and play! In addition, most of the children said they wished that all the people of the village, young and old, would get together to know each other better, preferably at lots of parties and barbecues. Food for thought indeed.

At the turn of the last century Tealing folk largely worked on the land and their main threat was illnesses like scarlet fever and diphtheria, which claimed many lives, young and old.

Nowadays the concerns are very different. The single biggest issue of concern to local people is the need for safety enhancements on the A 90 dual carriageway that runs right through the village. Before it was a dual carriageway, between 1959 and 1961, the road was dubbed" death mile" after six people were killed in accidents over that short period. The dual carriageway is better able to cope than the old road with the much heavier volume of traffic today. However, the lack of deceleration lanes for all the exits along the Tealing stretch and the absence of a safe pedestrian crossing contributes to the persistently high accident rate.

In October 1997, the tragic death of seventeen-year old local lad Greg Taylor as he tried to cross the A 90 on his bicycle, polarised local opinion and revived the campaign for safety enhancements. Since then, Greg's mother Lynne Taylor and the Community Council have campaigned tirelessly on the issue. Speaking to the Evening Telegraph after a recent serious accident near the spot where Greg died, Lynne said "underpasses and flyovers are needed and I would love to see a cut in the speed limit. I use the Tealingl Auchterhouse junction all the time and sometimes it is horrendous trying to join the main road. It only takes one impatient driver to cause a crash. It's too late for Greg, but I have a fifteen year old daughter and I just hope that something can eventually be done". Following the visit of the Scottish Office Minister of Transport to Tealing in 1998, speed cameras and improved signage were installed, but these measures fall far short of what local people feel is required, so the campaigning will continue.

Other issues are also of concern to local people as Tealing enters the millennium. Community Councillor Moira Paton is extremely keen to see environmental improvements in the Inveraldie area and on the site once occupied by Discovery Pallets. She points out that when Dundee District Council took over the administration of Tealing in the seventies, they published a report stating that landscaping, tree screening and verge improvement were urgently needed, but nothing was done. Moira said "the dereliction just south of Inveraldie is becoming a real eyesore and spoils the beauty of the landscape. Such a mess shouldn't be permitted in a nice rural spot. It's a great pity and we are hopeful that the local council will take it in hand to secure improvement".

Concerns also exist about the long-term outlook for Tealing Church. Although, closed and secure, the church is historically significant for it's background, ancient inscriptions and carvings. Many local people would like to see those preserved and, although ownership of the Church has reverted to the Crown, they are hopeful that something can be done to secure the future of the building.

Also, farmers in Tealing are experiencing the same downturn currently being felt in the farming industry throughout the UK. Charlie Young, owner of Sheilhill Farm, is hopeful that local farmers will see it through " the depression is currently hitting the area hard, but most of them are holding on" he said.

In 1968 the Rev James Kidd said that it would be interesting to see how community spirit in the village would survive the decline in the church and the increase in the number of commuter residents. He pondered whether incomers would want the same level of involvement in community life as those who live and work on the land. Thirty-two years later the question is still relevant, but much has changed, even in that period of time. People of all ages are now more mobile, more affluent and have a lot more choice about how they spend their free time. Within a 1S/20-minute drive of Tealing there are plenty of restaurants, clubs, shopping centres, leisure parks and theatres etc. More women are working and are having to juggle careers with the demands of family life and the home -and if they are working all day they are perhaps less inclined to leave the children in the evenings to attend adult community groups. Perhaps the way forward is to offer activities that all of the family can participate in together?

On the other hand, 21st century living is more independent and the rights of those who choose not to embrace village life must be respected. Everyone who chooses to live in Tealing enjoys the wonderful environment and quality of life it offers and it is inevitable that, for some, this is the sole attraction. As Secretary of the Community Council and an incomer myself, I've always felt welcome. And, like many other incomers, I've found the community spirit dramatically better in this wee country village than anything I have experienced before. But then, I am measuring it against anonymous city life, whereas those who have lived here for decades are comparing today with the halcyon days of the forties, fifties and sixties when Tealing was fairly "buzzing" with clubs, associations and camaraderie.

The other challenge is the physical distribution of the area. It is very spread out and contains several distinct "hamlets" and condensed areas of population that are almost small villages in themselves -Balgray, Kirkton, Inveraldie, Newbigging etc. This makes publicising village wide events and generally sharing information and community spirit that much more difficult, but not impossible.

The introduction to this book described Tealing as a "vibrant rural community with a rich and colourful past". That is exactly what Tealing is; and all who live, work and visit here, can be proud of that. Having survived pre-historic times, the Romans, the Picts, English invasion, several religious upheavals, two World Wars, farming depressions and all the other ups and downs of the last two thousand years, I think we can be confident that Tealing, the Gateway to Angus, will see many more millenniums. We certainly hope so!

This section tracks significant dates in the history of Tealing. For easy reference, it presents a snapshot of what has been chronicled in various books and journals through the ages, alongside updates from recent times.

100 AD	There is evidence of an early Pictish settlement in the area near a soutterain now known as Tealing Earthhouse, west of Tealing Home Farm
710	At the invitation of Nechtan, King of the Picts, the papal missionary Boniface comes to Scotland to help harmonise the Celtic Church with that of Rome. He founds churches at Invergowrie, Felin (Tealing) and Restenneth
1174	Hugh Giffard of Tealing is one of the hostages for the release of King William (the Lion) I of Scotland.
1175-1190	Hugh Giffard is popular at the court of William (the Lion) 1 of Scotland and is bestowed the grant of Tealing from the monarch. His eldest son is William Giffard and, together, they give the church of Tealing to the priory of St Andrews
1199	The priory of St Andrews is to hold the lands of Pitpointie, which had also been gifted to it by Hugh Giffard, as long as it holds the Church of Tealing
1275	The Church of Tealing is disjoined from the diocese of St Andrews and annexed to the diocese of Dunkeld. The parson of Tealing, in Roman Catholic and Episcopalian times, holds the office of Archdeacon of Dunkeld Cathedral
1380	The date of one of the earliest known piece of Scots inscription anywhere in Scotland. It was originally in the foundations of the old Tealing Church, and is now on the north wall inside the current church. Translated, it reads "Here lies Ingram of Kethenys, Priest, Master in Arts, Archdeacon of Dunkeldyn"
1409	Robert, Duke of Albany Regent, confirms the charter of the lands of Yester and Tealing by Euphamie Giffart, daughter and heir of the late Hugh Giffart, to Dungall McDowale

1427	Dungallas Makdowal, by Charter at Rossie Priory, records the transfer of the Barony of Telyn (Tealing) to his blood relative Eustace Maxwell, son of Sir William Maxwell of Caerlaverock, and husband of Agnes, daughter of Sir John Gifford (descendant of Hugh Giffard) Eustace is the first Maxwell of Tealing
1430	The House at Tealing is owned successively through the 1400s by the Maxwell family. At this stage it is probably a fortified house in the style of the later Powrie Castle
1445	Robert (or James) Maxwell of Tealing is slain fighting on the side of the Ogilvies at the Battle of Arbroath
1483	William Maxwell of Tealing is one of the jury at a retour (inheritance) of service of John Carnegie of Kinnaird
1508	Thomas Maxwell of Tealing is Sheriff Depute of Forfar
1508	Sir William Maxwell of Tealing, Knight, is one of the assize at the service of John Carnegie of Kinnaird
1553	Alexander Maxwell of Tealing, Magistrate, is charged with reset and the freeing of the thief, Andro Cosyne
1561	Adam Fowlie becomes Minister of Tealing Parish Church
1567	Andrew Gibb becomes Minister of Tealing Parish Church
1572	Alexander Maxwell of Tealing, along with his son and heir David and other local lairds, is charged with reset and intercommuning with rebels
1575	Alexander Maxwell of Tealing dies and is laid to rest in Tealing Churchyard
1584	Elizabeth, daughter of the late Thomas Maxwell of Tealing, marries Gilbert Strachan, the younger, of Claypotts
1590	John Ramsay becomes Minister of Tealing Parish Church
1595	Tealing Dovecot is built by Sir David Maxwell, it features his coat of arms and that of his wife, Lady Helen Maxwell of Tealing
1600	The Tealing House (that still exists today) is under construction and the original Tealing Home Farmhouse is built
1600	The chapel in the grounds of Tealing House is demolished and consecrated stones, taken from it, are built into the walls of the new Tealing Farmhouse for ornamental purposes

1601	Sir David Maxwell of Tealing is one of the four parties to approve of the weddings of sisters Isabella and Helen Strachan of Carmyllie (the daughters of Isabel Maxwell)
1609	Hugh Maxwell inherits the lands and Barony of Tealing from his father Sir David Maxwell
1618	Archdeacon of Dunkeld, John Ramsay, dies and his magnificent tombstone is placed in Tealing Church, where it remains today
1623	Alexander Bruce becomes Minister of Tealing Parish Church
1631	Patrick Maxwell inherits the Barony of Tealing from his father George Maxwell
1639	Lady Helen Maxwell of Tealing, widow of Sir David Maxwell, dies and is laid to rest in Tealing Graveyard. Her gravestone bears the arms of the Maxwell, Barclay, Gordon and Ogilvy families.
1648	Sir Patrick Maxwell , son of George Maxwell of Newark, inherits the church land called Prieston of Tealing and the tithes in the Parish of Tealing
1650	John Campbell becomes Minister of Tealing Parish Church
1665	Patrick Makgill becomes Minister of Tealing Parish Church
1682	Tealing House is described as a "good house, well planted and good yards" by Ochterlony
1684	John Lyon becomes Minister of Tealing Parish Church
1693	Thomas Maxwell of Tealing dies and is laid to rest in Tealing Churchyard
1694	Sir Patrick Maxwell of Tealing inherits the lands and Barony of Tealing from his father Sir Patrick Maxwell
1701	Sir Patrick Maxwell of Tealing dies and the male line fails. George Napier of Kilmahon makes up a crown title and succeeds as heir to Tealing
1704	George Napier makes over the barony of Tealing to John Scrymscure (late Provost of Dundee) and his son, also called John Scrymscure
Early 1700s	A major extension is installed to the central N face of Tealing House
1708	Hugh Maxwell becomes Minister of Tealing Parish Church

1719-1728	The Rev. John Glas is Minister of Tealing Parish Church
1728	The Rev. John Glas is suspended by the Synod of Angus & Mearns and later forms a breakaway church known as the Glassites, creating one of the greatest upheavals in the history of the Scottish church
1730	An artificial cave or subterraneous passage, also known as a weem, is discovered a little west of Tealing House, and is covered up
1731	John Stewart becomes Minister of Tealing Parish Church
1760	The sandy hillock on the farm of Balkemback, within the circle of large round stones that evidence a Druidical temple, is opened up and reveals stone coffins and early human remains
1761	Patrick Scrymsoure of Tealing marries Isobel Coutts of the celebrated Coutts banking family
1764	John Gellatly becomes Minister of Tealing Parish Church
1780	The Water Mill, known as the Old Mill, is built adjacent to the Tealing Burn at Tealing Home Farm. Not long afterwards, the road bridge over Tealing Burn is built just along the road.
1781	John Stewart becomes Minister of Tealing Parish Church
1790	An ancient subterraneous building of very irregular construction is discovered on the farm of Prieston
1797	Walter Tait becomes Minister of Tealing Parish Church
1803	Tealing Church manse is built
1806	Old Tealing Church is demolished and antiquities, taken from it, are built into the replacement church
1808	The Tealing Church (that still stands today) is built
1814	Charles Aidie becomes Minister of Tealing Parish Church
1815	Patrick Scrymsoure of Tealing dies, aged 66 years, and his estate goes to his son-in-law James Fothringham of Powrie (husband of his daughter Marion) who then takes the name of Scrymsoure Fothringham
1822	Isobel Scrymsoure, wife of Patrick Scrymsoure dies aged 61 years

1823	James Scott, mason, builds a semi-sunken ice house on the east bank of Tealing burn near Tealing Home Farm, for the preservation of meat and other supplies
1826	Tealing Home Farm farmhouse is converted to stables and coach house by James Pirnie, mason.
1827	George Tod becomes Minister of Tealing Parish Church
1827-29	Tealing House is extended and" aggrandised" by Mr William Burn, under the supervision of Mr James Black of Dundee
1830	Peter Balfour becomes Minister of Tealing Parish Church
1835	David Barclay Mellis becomes Minister of Tealing Parish Church
1837	James Scrymsoure Fothringham of Tealing and Powrie, dies aged 52 years
1843	The Free Church in Tealing is built on a site on the Huntingfaulds Road, Minister David Barclay Mellis
1843	William Elder becomes Minister of Tealing Parish Church
1861	Duncan Turner becomes Minister of the Free Church in Tealing
1862	Walter Thomas Scrymsoure Fothringham, son of Colonel Thomas Frederick Scrymsoure Fothringham is born in Algiers, Africa
1864	Colonel Thomas Frederick Scrymsoure Fothringham dies aged 27
1871	Tealing Earth House is discovered by local geologist and estate land steward, Mr Walter McNicoll
1873	Compulsory education at Tealing Public School is established
1875	Mrs Marion Fothringham Scrymsoure dies in Nice, France and is buried in the family vault at the Murroes
1883	Neil S Elder becomes Minister of the Free Church in Tealing
1884	Walter Thomas James Scrymsoure Fothringham comes of age and becomes proprietor of the estate of Powrie Tealing
1889	Samuel Macaulay becomes Minister of Tealing Parish Church
1908	The Tealing Geologist, Mr Walter McNicoll dies aged 81 years. His obituary and remembrance is presided over by the Rev Elder of the Tealing United Free Church
1909	The Tealing Bazaar is commemorated in poetry by Mr H Lamont
1909	Tealing Women's Guild is established

1913	Tealing Parish Hall, on a site diagonally opposite the Old Schoolhouse in the sharp bend on the Tealing Aucherhouse Road, opens with a concert and a dance to celebrate the event
1913	Robert Don (of the Don Brothers Buist family) occupies Tealing House and later dedicates a memorial seat in Tealing to the memory of his two sons who died during World War I
1921	The Tealing War Memorial is unveiled at a Dedication Service presided over by Rev D S Macaulay
1923	Tealing House is occupied by Edmund C Cox of the Dundee jute family
1924	Tealing WRI is established
1925	Ian Forbes McCulloch becomes Minister of Tealing Parish Church
1929	The Tealing Free Church closes and the congregation merges to worship at Tealing Parish Church
1929	James Alexander Sutherland Wilson becomes Minister of Tealing Parish Church
1930	Walter Thomas James Scrymsoure Fothringham dies and the estate is inherited by his son Thomas Steuart Fothringham, Esquire of Powrie Fothringham and Tealing
1937	The "Coronation Gate" at Petterden, and the nearby land featuring a roundel of trees, is donated to the Tealing Community by the Fothringham family to commemorate the Coronation of King George VI and Queen Elizabeth
1937	The estate of Tealing is sold to the Department of Agriculture, for £23,497, to meet the death duties of Thomas Steuart Fothringham
1938	The Department of Agriculture leases the land in Tealing for 41 small holdings
1939-45	The Tealing Home Guard meets at the Tealing Hall
1940	Tealing House is used as billets for the WAFFs
1941	Emmanuel Wood becomes Minister of Tealing Parish Church
1942	No 56 RAF Officer Training Unit moves from Sutton Bridge to the Tealing Aerodrome

1942	The Russian General, Molotov, lands at Tealing Airfield in a TB7 four engined aircraft, on a military mission to see Churchill
1942	The Reverend Edmund Parke becomes RAF Chaplain at Tealing
1945	The RAF Unit at Tealing is disbanded and is placed on care and maintenance under the wing of RAF Montrose
1945-88	Tealing House is owned by Mr William Bowie and a successful market garden is operated in the grounds
1947	The Old Tealing Hall is burned to the ground
1949	The present Tealing Hall is opened on Feb 9th. It had previously been used as a gymnasium, cinema and chapel for the servicemen and women from the aerodrome
1949	Charles Hugh Brew Harkness becomes Minister of Tealing Parish Church
1953	Tealing celebrates the Coronation of Queen Elizabeth the 11 with a full day of events including a sports tournament, a fancy dress parade for the children and a slap up meal in the village hall. The festivities are recorded on cine film for posterity
1954	The council houses are built in Inveraldie and many of the tenants move out of the old RAF huts into the new houses
1958	William Charles Smith becomes Minister of Tealing Parish Church #
1962	James Kidd becomes Minister of Tealing Parish Church
1963	Tealing parish church is linked with Murroes Church under the Ministry of Rev. J Kidd
1972	Tealing Primary School celebrates its centenary and one hundred years of compulsory schooling in Scotland, by staging a "Victorian" school exhibition
1975	Tealing becomes part of the District of the City of Dundee, having previously been in the jurisdiction of Angus County Council
1983	Tealing Parish Church closes when the congregations of Tealing and Murroes unite and worship moves to Murroes Parish Church
1985	The dual carriageway (now the A90) through Tealing opens
1988	Mr G Thomson becomes the owner of Tealing House
1996	Due to local government re-organisation, Tealing returns to the

jurisdiction of Angus Council

1998	Calum McDonald, Scottish Office Minister for Transport, visits Tealing in response to the Tealing Community Council Campaign for safety enhancements
1998	Improved signage, warning of pedestrians, is installed on the A 90
1999	Speed cameras are installed on the stretch of the A 90 through Tealing
1999	"Gateway" and "drive safely" signage is installed on the Tealing/ Auchterhouse Road through the village
1999	Nursery education is offered at Tealing Primary School for the first time
2000	The people of Tealing, with their family and friends come together at Tealing Hall on 4 June 2000 to celebrate the Millennium. The Provost opens a new and permanent photographic exhibition of Tealing through the ages and this book is published. Several hundred people joined in the happy celebrations, the book sold out and a grand time was had by all!

BIBLIOGRAPHY

Memorials of Angus and the Mearns, By Andrew Jervise, F.S.A. Scot

Published by David Douglas, Edinburgh, 1885
The Statistical Account of Scotland 1791-1799, edited by Sir John Sinclair, Angus, Volume XIII, EP Publishing Ltd

The New Statistical Account of Scotland, Vol 11, William Blackwood and Sons,

Edinburgh and London, 1845
The Third Statistical account of Scotland, Vol 26, edited by William Allen Illsley, M.A. PhD, Herald Press, Arbroath, 1977

The Angus and the Mearns Remembrancer 1845-1848 Ancient Church Dedications in Scotland Fasti Ecclesiae Scoticanae, Vols 5, 9 and 10, By Hew Scott, D.D

Published by Oliver and Boyd, Tweeddale Court Edinburgh, 1925 Bede's Ecclesiastical History Ordnance Gazetteer of Scotland, Vol 6, edited by Francis H Groome, assistant editor of

the "Globe Encyclopaedia" Published by Edinburgh: Thomas C Jack, publishing works,

London: 45 Ludgate Hill. Glasgow: 48 Gordon Street. 1855.
Pre 1855 Gravestone Inscriptions in Angus
Listed by Sydney Cramer, Alison Mitchell and Adam Tudor-Hart

Notice Regarding a Picts House at Tealing by Andrew Jervise, FSA Scot, June 1873

Angus or Forfarshire, the Land and the People, Vols 1-5, By Alex J Warden, F.S.A.Scot
Published by Charles Alexander & Co, Dundee 1880 Notice of Prehistoric Remains near Tealing in Forfarshire by J Romilly Allen, FSA Scot,

Feb 1881 The Baronage of Angus and the Mearns, By David MacGregor Peter. Published by Oliver and Boyde, Tweeddale Court, Edinburgh. Alex Rodgers, High Street, Montrose.

Epitaphs and Inscriptions Vol1 and 2 By Andrew Jervise, F.S.A., published by David Douglas, Edinburgh, 1879

Tealing School Board Minutes 1872-1919
Hillside Musings by James C Purgavie
Published by James P. Mathew 1900

Annals of the Free Church of Scotland, by the Rev W Ewing, 1914

The Family of Cox in Angus & Perthshire by William Henry Cox of Snaigow, published by Harry K Cox General Register of Sasines, County of Forfar, Thomas Steuart Fothringham Esquire of

Fothringham and Tealing, 17 Nov 1937

Action Stations, Military Airfields of Scotland, the North-East, and Northern Ireland by David J Smith, published by Patrick Stephens, Cambridge Tealing Parish Statutory List, Angus Council The Courier and Evening Telegraph -various articles Symbolstone by Alistair D Carty -http://forteviot.symbolstone.org http://members.aol.com/ skyelander/ www.ufcos.org.uk

L - #0164 - 240321 - C0 - 210/148/4 - PB - DID3051122